Written by Crona Temple

Cover design by Tina DeKam
Cover illustration by Dan Burr
First published in 1879
This version is unabridged.
© 2021 Jenny Phillips
goodandbeautiful.com

Table of Contents

Chapter 1
ANTONY'S TRIALS

Is there no hope, Doctor?"

The speaker was a stalwart fisherman, who stood bareheaded beside the doctor's horse. His rough voice shook with emotion, and his hand clutched the bridle like a vice, as he awaited the answer to his question: "Is there no hope?"

"I fear not," was the reply, "I fear not: your wife is blind; I can do nothing more for her. It is a heavy affliction, but you must remember, Antony, that at one time we feared for her very life; instead of grieving, you ought to be thankful it is no worse. It's wonderful how soon folks get to do without their eyesight."

Dr. Doran was a kind-hearted man, and the words he spoke were intended to be kind and comforting, but they missed their mark widely now. Antony did not even seem to hear them; his hand dropped from the bridle rein as if his arm had been suddenly paralyzed; he stood quite still where the doctor had left him gazing straight before him across the strip of moorland, out to the horizon line of the stormy sea. He was but an Irish fisherman—rude, uneducated, and poor—yet he had a brave, affectionate heart beating beneath his coarse jersey; uneducated as he was, he had learned lessons from God's waves and storms, from God's mountains sleeping beneath the silent stars, lessons which many wise men, with all their boasted booklore, are ignorant of. Poor as he was—in one sense of the term—yet he had riches which are worth thousands of gold and silver, even a humble, contented spirit and a childlike, trusting faith.

He stood there to wrestle awhile with his trouble, heedless of the rising wind which came rushing down the mountain gorges and of the raindrops which the blast began to dash in his face. The seagulls flew screaming above him, and the brook beside him leaped noisily over its stony bed, but he only heard one sound—the echo of the doctor's words, "your wife is blind."

"So it's the truth, that it is," he said at last, "and she will sit no more on the rocks to watch for the boat a-coming in. Her bright bonnie eyes will shine into my heart no more. Blind! That's what she is—blind! Darkness, and darkness always." His voice sank away almost to a groan; and sitting down on a rock, he covered his face with his hands, while big tears forced their way between his toil-stained fingers.

Antony Creigan had lived, as his forefathers had done, on a "farm" by the seashore. He had his two-roomed cottage; his one or two cows; his patches of potatoes, oats, and barley; and his moorland acres of coarse pasturage. Beside this, he had his boat—a crazy old yawl, with sundry tokens of repairs upon her sides, as well as upon her sails; yet he and his neighbor Patrick Boner had brought many a cargo of fish to the little quay and had earned thereby no inconsiderable addition to their means of subsistence. To the minds of the primitive people of the remote corner of Donegal in which Antony lived, he appeared quite a wealthy man; and Margaret Boyd was considered quite a blessed girl when he asked her to be his wife.

Margaret, or "Madge," as she was generally called, thought so too. She was very young—many years younger than Antony—a pretty, heedless child; and though she brought him no "fortune," not even a cow, she brought him what he reckoned dower enough and to spare: the brightness of her loving smile and the music of her laugh and of her song.

They had lived eight years in their cottage on the hillside, the desolate moorlands stretched out behind them and the sea broken by long, bold headlands lying to the west. No strangers ever came to Glenderg: "the neighbors" were poor and ignorant as themselves. There was a rude Roman Catholic chapel on the other side of the mountain, and miles beyond there was the little Protestant church, to which Antony would ride his rough black pony, with Margaret sometimes perched behind him, her arm round her husband's waist, her prayer-book—which she could not read—carefully wrapped in a red handkerchief on her knee. Antony went to church, for he said, "it was the least he could do to show a bit of respect to the good God who was over all"; but only a few of his Protestant neighbors followed his example. The church was far away; the clergyman, aged and infirm, could not come to visit the scattered cottages of Glenderg; and, in consequence, this distant corner of the parish seemed totally neglected and forgotten. Yet in the fisherman's home, the light of love and truth shone bright and clear, and Antony continued daily to spell out some portion of God's holy word, with his wife and babies gathered around him. Occasionally some of the neighbors would drop in and reverently listen while Antony would read some of the precious promises, the teachings, and the doctrines which have been hidden from the wise and prudent, and revealed unto the simple-minded ones.

But dark days were coming for Glenderg. A raging fever broke out among the people: many sickened and died. The hot summer sun beat remorselessly against the cliffs, and the ebb and flow of the pure, salt sea could not carry off the decaying heaps of seaweed and wrack which the winter's storms had driven so high up on the shore. The cottages were ill-ventilated and dirty; and in spite of Dr. Doran's efforts, it was long before Death had gathered in his last sheaf, and the pestilence was stayed. Little John Creigan, Antony's eldest and most fondly loved child, was one of the first to die; his brother Philip followed him, leaving to the bereaved parents only Dennis and little Madge in their sorrowful home. And though the father's eyes were full of scalding tears as he stood above his boys' open grave, he said to himself as he turned homewards: "I have much yet left to me, praised be God; and I know rightly it is all well now with the children. They have a home beyond there, better nor our poor house by the sea; and the knowledge of them up above will be a chain, like, to drag us up to heaven, too."

But sad news awaited him on his return to Glenderg. They met him on the way and told him his wife had been stricken, and he found her with the flush upon her cheek and the glassy eyes which had already wrung his heart with agony when he had marked the symptoms during the time preceding the death of his two brave boys. For many days he tended her almost in despair. "God's hand is very weighty on me," he groaned. "It is more than I can suffer: let me die with her, for to lose her is more than I can bear."

But Margaret did not die: for long she battled with the fierce fever which had claimed so many victims; and it was not till the summertime was past, and the clear sharp breezes blew again from off the sea, that the sickness relaxed its hold, and Creigan clasped his wife in his arms and knew that the danger was past. The reaction from the depth of his despair made him sorely repent his past murmurings. He felt as if he could never again doubt the goodness and love of God, as if the earnest service of his whole life would be but a faint and worthless proof of the sincerity of his gratitude.

As if to put him to the test, yet another trial was laid upon him. One day Dr. Doran beckoned him out of the house and told him that the blindness, which they had hoped was only temporarily affecting his wife's eyesight, was becoming a very serious matter—that it was entirely baffling his skill and that he feared the very worst results.

"Do you mean that she'll see no more, sir?" asked Creigan in a choking voice.

"I cannot say certainly now," was the answer; "but I shall be here again on Thursday, and then I can tell you. It is sad that in this wild place we cannot get a second opinion: another doctor's advice I mean."

"Oh, sir, would that help ye? As it is, I must sell the cows, but there's the boat and the tenant-right of the land, and I would be only too thankful—"

"No, no, my poor fellow," interrupted the kindly doctor, "it would be no use: a hundred doctors could do no good, if it is as I fear with her eyes. I only wished for another opinion just for my own satisfaction. Go back to her now, and don't say anything about it until I come on Thursday."

And now it was Thursday; the last sad confirmation had been given; Dr. Doran had said: "I can do nothing more: your wife is blind."

"My poor Madge! My poor Madge, and are ye never more to look upon the blessed sun or to spy the wee bits of flowers coming peepin' from the bog? Nor race with the childer round the hill when ye hear me shoutin' on the strand? Ay, it's hard to bear! It's hard to bear!"

A child's voice spoke beside him, and a child's little hand was laid upon his knee.

"Father, the storm is rising, and it is getting dark; come in. Mother is sleeping, and Dennis and me is lonely all by ourselves."

"Ay, wee one, I'll come," he answered, but he did not stir.

"What for were you cryin', father?" said little Madge, after a pause. "You tell us John and Phil are right happy where they've gone to; and we have mother now, though Paddy Boner's ones have lost their mammy, and so has Nelly Connel. So why did you cry, father? Sure it's not for Johnnie or Phil, and it can't be for mother."

It all came to him then, the consciousness of his rebelliousness and the murmurings: it was fit he should be rebuked by the lips of his child. "Indeed, yes, why was I cryin' and frettin'? The childer and I can be as eyes to her here, and if, in Christ's mercy, we reach the heavenly shore, then, for certain, she'll have her dear eyes again; for there they all 'see His face.'" And he went towards the house, carrying little Madge in his arms, and softly repeating: "They need no candle, nor the light of the sun, for the Lord Himself will give them light."

Chapter 2
THE OCTOBER STORM

Margaret was not sleeping when her husband entered the cottage. She lifted her head when she heard his step. "Come here, Anton dear, I want to speak till ye. Tell me why the doctor spoke so pitiful to me the day, and the last time he was here; and why are ye so quiet and whist like? Is there anything the matter ye haven't tel't me about?"

How could he answer her? He knelt down beside the rude bedstead on which she was lying and looked into her face. The ravages of the fever had sadly changed her; her cheeks looked hollow and pallid; her hair, the black hair Antony was so proud of, had all been cut closely off, but the beautiful eyes were beautiful still, the long lashes veiling the bright blue which is so marked a characteristic of the western Irish. But in Margaret's eyes now there was a strained, pathetic expression, which went to Antony's heart.

"What is it?" she asked him again, "what ails us?"

"Are ye weary of the darkness, ahaska[1]?" he said, very low.

"Then it is true!" she exclaimed. "Oh, Antony, did ye think

---

1   darling

I didn't notice the way the doctor has been touching my eyes this long while past? D'ye think I couldn't tell by the very tones of yer voice that something was grieving you sore? Don't fret yourself to me, for I know already that I am blind."

"Oh, Madge, Madge!"

"Hust ye! hust ye! There is no need to take on about it: the good God, aye, fits the back for the burdthen, ye know. I'm a bit weak after the fever, or I'd make you take heart, Antony. It isn't you that is used to be downcast: cheer up; indeed, and I'll do finely after a bit."

There was reverence mingling with love in the kiss Antony laid on his wife's brow. "God help me!" he said. "Ye're braver and truer than I, Madge; I'm not fit for to tread in your shadow, let alone to stand by your side. Wee Madge counted up my blessings to me outside there, a minute agone; and now you, you on whom the brunt of the sorrow falls, you bid me take heart and trust the Lord."

"Ay, to be sure, and why wouldn't I? I have been thinking on some words ye read once out of the Book, Antony; something about the good God leading the blind with His own hand, and making twisting things straight for them, and the black darkness all bright; do you remember whereabouts it is? I'm a bit tired now, and I'd like to hear ye read it before I sleep."

But Antony looked for a long time in vain; he was not, as he himself would have phrased it, "over much of a scholar," and he turned over the pages of the Bible, one by one, with small hope of finding the verse which his wife had asked for, but he lighted on these words and read them to her: "He shall give His angels charge over thee, to keep thee in all thy ways. They shall bear thee up in their hands, lest thou dash thy foot against a stone;" and, secure in the promise of heavenly protection and love, Margaret sank to sleep.

It was not until his wife and children had long been soundly slumbering, and when the firelight was beginning to burn low and to fail him, that Antony found the words he was searching for; they were these: "I will bring the blind by a way that they knew not; I will lead them in paths that they have not known; I will make darkness light before them, and crooked things straight. These things will I do unto them, and not forsake them." And then again, a few pages farther on: "Who is among you that feareth the Lord, that obeyeth the voice of His servant, that walketh in darkness, and hath no light? Let him trust in the name of the Lord, and stay upon his God." He read them over and over, sitting there in the flicker of the firelight, the wind howling and rushing around the rudely-built cabin, and the thunder of the waves on the beach sounding like a cannonade of heavy guns.

The voice of the tempest seemed to him as the voice of God: the God who "holdeth the waters in the hollow of His hand," who "maketh the clouds His chariot and walketh upon the wings of the wind." And this powerful One, this Ruler and Controller of earth's vastest forces, was the God who had promised "never to forsake," who had bidden the fainting soul to trust in His name.

Comforted and happy, Antony Creigan lay down to rest.

It had been a wild night! And now with the morning, instead of decreasing, the storm seemed to be gathering fresh force; the waves rose higher against the cliffs; and at the head of the bay, where a narrow beach was generally to be seen, was nothing but a stretch of froth and spray; the huge waves rushed in like live creatures, endowed with uncontrollable rage and fury, and flung themselves on the sand; but they could not sweep back again in the teeth of the westerly gale; so every moment the furious sea, gathering in volume, threatened destruction to the few poor huts built just above high-water mark. The people had spent an anxious night, not one of them had slept; and while the Creigans rested peacefully in their cottage on the hillside, their neighbors with frightened faces gathered on the shore, many of them calling on the Virgin and the saints for assistance and preservation. Higher and higher rose the tide; but the daylight had come at last, the ebb would soon commence, and the cottagers of Glenderg felt the peril was past.

But now, mingling with the raging of the storm and the roar of the waters, came another sound; they listened. It came again and again, the unmistakable boom of a distant gun, the signal of a ship in distress! Every one hurried to the heights above the strand, but the air was full of driving spray and of flying froth and spume; they could see nothing; while over and again came the sudden hollow sound, the "minute gun at sea." Antony Creigan had heard it, and, like the rest, he climbed to the cliffs on the south side of the bay. It was a strange scene: men wild and eager, women with bare feet and red kerchiefs tied over their tossed hair, half-grown lads and little children—some yet pale and wan from the sickness they had so lately struggled with, all in the maddest excitement, shouting and gesticulating—yet now and then standing silently listening, trying to distinguish from the sound of the gun which way the doomed vessel was driving. But their anxious watching, their excited clamor arose from no feeling of pity for the fellow creatures now at the mercy of the cruel sea. Their hopes, their longings were not for the delivery, but for the destruction of the ship, that they might plunder the wreck.

It was awful, no doubt, but pause before you blame the poor villagers of Glenderg too severely. Consider their life—ignorant and neglected—paying yearly their tiny rental, which, small as it was, had been hardly scraped together from their scanty resources. Their fish, their seaweed, their butter, and their eggs: these were all they had to depend on. They worked in their fields, but only to raise crops enough for their own consumption, for there was no market for hay, corn, or even potatoes. What marvel, then, that they looked on a wreck as a godsend? What marvel that hopelessness and apathy should

change into exultant joy at the terrible sound of the "minute
gun"?

Antony had learned something more than his neighbors
knew, something which he had read in his Book by his
fireside, and he remembered how our Saviour had stood before
fishermen as poor and needy as Himself, and before grasping
scribes and purse-proud Pharisees, and had said: "As ye would
that men should do to you, do ye also to them likewise. . . . Be
ye merciful as your Father also is merciful." And Antony glanced
at the faces of the crowd, and though no word passed his lips,
nor no direct prayer was formed in his head, an aspiration went
up to heaven, not unlike that most Divine and most sacred one
ever recorded: "Father, forgive them, for they know not what
they do."

A man spoke to him; it was big Shan O'Donnel, of Ennis
Point. "I say, Anton man, she's safe to strike before the hour's
out! What think ye?"

"No ship wrought by human hands can live much longer
in yon sea," he returned. "It seems almost wrong to pray for it,
like."

"Pray for her to get clear off, is it? Are ye fair mad, Antony?
Why should ye be praying away the bread from the children's
mouths, the work from our idle hands? Has the fever left ye so
strong up at your house that ye can pray the likes of that?"

"Ay, it may bring us bread, surely; but think of the poor
creatures aboard of her! Think of—"

"Hoot, man! Ye said yersel', this minute, she was boun' to
strike; and won't it be better for her to come in here till us, than
weather Forman Head, and be driven right across Donegal Bay,
off to the coast of Sligo? But, there she is, there! There!"

Antony looked and saw below the cliff, not a cable length
from the huge wall of stone, there, shrouded in mist and spray,
the fated ship. One mast was still standing; the others had
long been carried away. Strips of the tattered sails still hung to

the yards, and one shred of scarlet bunting blew wildly in the
wind. She seemed to be waterlogged, for she was very deep in
the water; and the huge waves rolling up behind her, poured
themselves continually upon her decks. Not a living creature
could be discerned, and the gun had been silent for a long time
now. On she came, straight for the cliff, urged by wind and wave
with terrific force. The crowd on the shore held their breath—it
was, in truth, a fearful sight to see! Just opposite, there was a
long narrow cleft, running far into the wall of rock; and into
this sharp chasm the ship was swept. A huge billow came rolling
in; it lifted the ship on its mighty crest—lifted her high, as if
she had been but a feather weight, and hurled her against the
cliff. Another wave came leaping in—a third—and then the good
barque lay a mere mass of broken, tossing driftwood on the
surface of the triumphant sea.

Chapter 3
SAVED FROM THE SEA

There was fine plunder for Glenderg strewn over the bay, and some of the men perilled their very lives, stretching after a beam of wood, a cask, or package, which was tossing in the boiling waters. Soon the coast guardsmen appeared and took possession in the Queen's name, until the ship's history could be discovered and the usual legalities and forms gone through. Antony returned homewards hurriedly to tell his wife of the wreck and to see if any one could be found to stay with her during his absence; for he intended to return to Ennis Head to have his share in the work of "salvage": work which would bring him some of the money he needed so sadly just now.

He came springing down the hillside, as fast as the buffeting winds would allow him, for every hour was precious; only his strong love for his suffering wife could have made him leave the bustling scene of work and danger there at the wreck. On the other side of the narrow valley stood his cottage, halfway up the slope of the opposite hill; and between lay the scattered huts comprising the village

of Glenderg, skirting the now deserted beach. Along this
beach he strode rapidly, and was just about to turn off into
the direct route to his home, when he perceived some dark
objects lying at the extreme end, where the strand ended in
the abrupt sides of the headland which formed the north
side of the bay. A few moments more, and he had reached
the spot. He saw a boat—or rather, the fragments of one—
beaten and broken by the force of the sea—beyond, another
boat, which seemingly had met with more gentle usage; and
between them was a tangled mass of sails and spars and the
stiff form of a sailor, lying with his dead white face upturned
and the death-film over his awful eyes.

Antony knelt beside him and tore aside his shirt, which
alone covered his chest; but the experienced eye of the
fisherman saw at once that help had come too late: there was
the mark of a frightful blow across the temple, which alone
would have been sufficient to take his life. He laid the body
where the waves could not reach and reverently covered it
with a sail, placing large stones so as to prevent the wind
stripping off the temporary shelter. It was evident that the
unfortunate crew had taken to the boats when they perceived
the iron-bound shore on which they were being driven. But
they had only turned from one death to another! The waves
had swamped their frail cockleshells, crushed and broken
them, and cast them up on the strand, roaring and hissing as
it dashed them there, as if glorying in its ruthless work.

Antony turned away; but as he turned, he caught sight
of a heap of something white upon a piece of wreck. It was
a child—a little girl, apparently about six years old, bound
securely to a spar. He cut away the ropes and unknotted the
black silk handkerchief, which was passed carefully around
her waist and touching the little form with loving hands.

"It is dead, I doubt—the poor, tender lamb! The dear life is
fairly beaten out of its pretty breast! The wee hands are cold

as death, but it cannot lie here in the storm;" and he lifted
her gently in his strong arms, clasping the little hands in his
own big brown ones, and parting the hair—dripping as it was
with sea water—tenderly from off the sweet white face; and he
bore her, as her own mother might have done, away from the
thunder of the surf, away from the beating of the blast, to his
cottage on the hill.

Was it his fancy merely? Or did the child's limbs really
quiver as he held them in his arms? Did the eyelids really
partly unclose with some faint sign of returning life?

Yet faster Antony Creigan ran on, the very idea that he
might be able to save the life that had ebbed so far, lent wings
to his feet. He dashed open his door—

"See, Madge, woman! see what I've brought ye!" And then,
suddenly recollecting himself, he said, sadly: "I've found a
wee gisseh[1] lying near drownded on the strand; give me yer
hand, Madge, and feel her pretty face. There is life in her yet,
I b'lieve; and, please God, we will bring her to, again. Oh, but
I wish ye could see the beautiful face of her!"

Margaret raised herself on her elbow and bade him lay
the child beside her upon the bed. It was touching to see
her, blind and ill as she was, forgetting her affliction and her
weakness, as she chafed the tiny limbs and unfastened the
saturated clothing.

"Madgie," she called, "open the big chest beside the
window, and find my shawl—make hurry, dear! Hold it close
to the fire, and get it brave and hot."

"But, mother," objected the little Madge, "sure this is yer
red shawl, yer Sunday one!"

"Ay, it is thicker and warmer than aught else in the house.
Be quick, child!"

Antony had poured whiskey into the palms of his hands
and was rubbing the fiery liquid over the benumbed body.

---

1   *girl*

"Ye poor darlint!" he murmured, "if yer mother could see ye now, she would be crazed with grief."

"Where are the rest, Antony?" asked his wife.

"Drownded: drownded every one of them! Oh, Madge, ye don't know what a fearsome storm it is."

"And the ship?"

"Scattered out like a bundle of reeds cast loose over the sea. She struck at the gully on Ennis Head; ye can guess what chance there was for her there."

"Oh, Anton! Why aren't ye there then? It's worth poun's and poun's, the first hours after a wreck."

"Could I stay without looking after ye a bit? And now that I've foun' this child, would ye allow me to leave her to perish without doin' my best for her?"

"Ah, if it was only the strength that I had! I could tend her without eyesight—Antony! Ten poun's of salvage money, and we needn't sell the cows at all, at all."

He ceased from his work of chafing and rubbing and laid his hand upon her shoulder. "Don't ye fret, alanna[2]! We shall pull through at last, never ye fear! The wean's life is worth more than the cows."

"True for ye, ye are right, surely," said his wife humbly, her sightless eyes filling with tears as she turned them toward his voice.

"Here, Madgie, child, make hot the shawl again; and mind, don't burn holes through it!" So Madge, important with the responsibility of her allotted task, held one end of the gaily checked garment, while Dennis, a toddling baby of two years old, supported the other, gazing all the while, with open-mouthed astonishment, at his parents, as they tended the fair-haired stranger lying there so very white and still.

It was not long before that deathlike stupor changed gradually into healthful sleep. A rose flush crept again to

---

2   *dearest*

tinge the lips and cheeks; and the delicate chest heaved with
gentle, regular breathings. "She is in a fair way to do good,
now, praised be God!" said Antony, with reverent glance
upward. And Margaret echoed, "Thank God"; yet she sighed
as she spoke the words.

"Now for a bite to eat, and I'll be off," said the father,
cheerfully, and he shared out some "oaten-cake" and
porringers of milk, for himself and the children, and carefully
prepared a cup of tea and some "white bread," for his wife.
Then charging "wee Madge to be good and mind Dennis,"
with a last glance at the rescued child, and a last word of love
to Margaret, he started to try and find one of the neighbors
to stay with his helpless household during his absence. In
this, something to his own surprise, he was successful: an old
woman, too old to go "a clambering and a scrambling over
them rocks" and yet quite able and willing to brave the storm
between her own house and Antony's, tucked her knitting
under her arm, and her cloak about her shoulders, and
promised him to take all under her charge: so, with a light
heart, and quick footstep, he once more took his way to the
shore, without one regretful thought of the time lost or of the
rich hauls of wreck-gear which had been made in his absence,
but with a thankful remembrance of the life he had snatched
from the jaws of death, and a brave looking forward to a
future of happiness, which was to be won by work, and by
love. It should not be his fault if his blind Margaret found her
darkness unendurable, or if she fancied her rude mountain
home was less comfortable than it had been in the happy
days before the fever came, with its train of sorrow and trial.
But whatever was in store for him, surely Antony Creigan had
learned to say from his heart, the sentence which is so often
but lip-deep: "God's will be done!"

Chapter 4
AGATHA

The wild storm sank away almost as suddenly as it had risen; the wind fell, and the heavy clouds rolled off beyond the mountains; only the sea could not be at rest. Far out on the horizon line, the huge waves rose like miniature hills against the sky; and along the shore, they dashed themselves with an incessant sobbing and wailing, as if wearied of their boisterous play.

The coastguard had removed the bodies of the poor drowned sailors, such, as least, as had been cast upon the shore, and coffins had been hastily knocked together, that they might be carried to the distant churchyard and rest peacefully in their nameless graves. Long lines of sea wrack lay along the beach, mingled with broken beams of wood and such-like fragments of the wreck—sad relics of the ship that had sailed so gaily in the sunshine, and cut so proudly through the billows, only two short days ago!

It was nearly midday when Antony Creigan approached his home. All night long he had been engaged, under the coastguard officer, in the work of "salvage," dragging anything

of value out of reach of the waves and guarding it while
on the shore from the depredations of his more lawless
neighbors. He was going to snatch a few hours' rest now, for
he was very weary. He had had much watching, and many
troubles lately; and even his strong frame felt the effects of
sleepless nights and anxious days. He was walking slowly and
painfully up the hill, when a glad shout made him raise his
head.

"Father! There's father!"

On a block of granite before the door was perched "wee
Madge"—a sentinel evidently on the look out for him; for
when she caught sight of him, she sprang to the ground and
rushed up to the threshold, where her little brother Dennis
stood by the side of a "creepy stool," on which sat the pretty
fair-haired child he had saved from the cruel sea. Madge
pointed him out proudly.

"See! That is father! Him as bringed you home yesterday."

The little one looked up at him with grave, grey eyes;
her clothing had been dried, but she still was wrapped
in Margaret's red shawl, and over it her yellow hair fell in
shining locks below her shoulders. She looked so unlike the
children beside her, so dignified, in her baby fashion, that
Antony involuntarily raised his hand to his cap as he asked,

"D'ye find yoursel' better this mornin', miss?"

"I wasn't ill, only the water took my breath away," she
answered him slowly, but immediately changing her tone
to one of intense eagerness, she demanded, "Have you seen
Captain Royston? Or Mr. Slade, or any of the men? Have you
told them I am here? And where is Catherine?"

Antony stood gazing at her, his face full of pitying
admiration; what answer could he give her? How was he to
tell her she alone had been preserved; that of all the good
ship's company, she only remained alive; that Captain
Royston and his men lay at this moment, stiff and cold, in the

coastguard's watchhouse on the shore?

"Do you not understand me?" asked the child again. "Won't you go and tell Catherine, or the Captain, that I am here?"

"Little lady," said he, gently, "I have seen nothing of 'Catherine'; who is she?"

"She is my nurse; she will be angry with me if I stay so long away from her. Why do you keep me here? She—" pointing to the cottage— "would not let me run down to the shore; she said you were coming soon and would bring Catherine, or Mrs. Royston, up here to me; where are they? Won't you tell somebody that I am here?"

"Oh, don't cry!" said Madgie, coming close up to her, "don't go for to cry! Father will bring them all here this minute, I know; won't you, father?"

"No, child, I cannot do that. Listen till me, dear, wee, lost wean! It's sorry I am to have to tell such news to ye, but it's the sair, said truth, it is, and ye must know it sooner or later. Not one, saving yersel', reached the strand with the life in them; I found ye strapped to a big baulk of timber, nearly as cold and dead as the poor drownded man by your side; and it was God's mercy led me over that end of the strand jest to save ye, for sure, in another half hour, the breath would have been gone entirely, without a bit of warmth or shelter. It was His will to save ye, my poor one! And 'twas His will that all them others should perish in the sea, and—"

She sprang up, seizing his arm in her terror and distress, "What do you say? Everybody drowned but me? Oh, Mr. Slade! Dear Mr. Slade! He is not dead! And surely the Captain is not dead, oh, no! It can't be, it can't be!"

Antony stooped down, and lifting the child in his arms, carried her, sobbing and struggling, into the cottage.

"Leave me alone, oh, leave me alone!" she cried, "I hate you! This is a horrible place, and you are a cruel man! Oh, let me go."

"Where is it ye want to go to, darlint?" he asked her gently; "there is no place more fitter, like, for ye hereabouts. I am very tired now, but tomorrow morning, please God, I will step over to the rectory and ask his riv'rence how to get ye home to your friends; be aisy now, ahaska, be aisy!"

He set her down in the most comfortable chair he could find and approached his wife. She was dressed for the first time since her illness and sitting on the side of her bed.

"Oh, you're welcome, Antony! I thought ye'd never come. The child has been calling out for ye to bring her one and another of they poor dead folks, until it has been fair heartbreaking to hear her. You have told it to her now, I reckon; how sore she is crying, poor lamb, poor lamb!"

"I must get some sleep, Madge; I am dead beat." He pulled some oaten straw from a sort of loft which stretched over half his cottage like a low ceiling (across the other half the smoke-stained rafters and thatch were visible), and spreading the straw on the floor beside the fire, he threw himself, drenched as he was, upon it, to rest and sleep if he could.

Margaret came slowly from her bed, feeling her dark way along the well-known walls and scanty furniture. She came across the threshold into the outer room, and bidding Madge and little Dennis run down to the sea awhile and amuse themselves, she softly approached the weeping child. She knelt beside her, partly because the exertion she had made had well nigh exhausted her feeble strength, and partly that she might bring her face close to that of her unwilling visitor.

"I'm afeared ye are very unhappy, my dear; but ye must not take on so. Do ye see Antony there? He is wet and tired, and he must sleep now: he carried ye up from the shore, and he tended ye like your own mother would have done, he was that tender and careful of you. Ye see I cannot do hardly a heate[1]

---

1   *a very little bit*

for you, because the Lord has taken away the use of my eyes."

The child raised her head. "Are you blind? I remember I heard that little girl say something about it, but I was not listening to her; I was watching for Catherine, or—oh, dear! Oh, dear!" and she began to cry afresh. But Margaret persevered.

"As I was telling ye," she went on, "my man, there, he did a power for ye, and now he is gettin' a bit of rest. You will not disturb him, darlin'? Whisht, whisht! I know what a sore heart is, myself: my two bonnie boys, that were the light of the house, have been laid in the black ground since Midsummer time; and my heart near broke with longing after them, but still I am happy when I think on them, though I miss them more, a'most now, than ever. So it is not because I don't know sorrow that I bid ye to cease cryin', but because I want ye to look on to the happy days a coming, as I strive to do."

Maybe Margaret's words were lost on her hearer, but the kindly tone had its effect; the sobs were stilled, though the big tears came trickling fast down the poor little cheeks, and the frightened look had not left the large grey eyes.

"It may not be good manners to ax ye, but will ye tell me yer name, darlin'?"

"Agatha Buchanan."

"Sure, and it is a fine name! I never heard the like so of it before. Now, Miss Agatha, will ye lie down with me on the childer's bed, if I make it pretty with spreading the shawl over it? Ye're trembling, poor darling, and I'm afeard I cannot stay here with ye any longer; ye see I'm not so strong now."

Agatha looked at her for the first time, and the patient expression of the beautiful sightless eyes found its way to her little heart.

"You lie down," she said. "Let me lead you to the bed. I will sit outside on the rock until you are rested."

"Better not, dear. Don't go in sight of yon sea again today. Won't ye jest lie yourself down here by my side, till Antony wakes?"

Now, in spite of herself, the child crept upon the rude pallet, and laying her fair head on the peasant woman's arm, wearied as she was, she soon fell fast asleep.

Chapter 5
THE CURATE'S ADVICE

Antony kept his word about going over to the rectory to enquire as to the best means to be taken for tracing out Agatha's "friends"; but he found the old clergyman was ill, too ill to see anyone or to attend to any business whatever. His duty in the church was to be performed by the curate of the next parish, which was fifteen miles away! If Creigan could wait until next Sunday for the advice he asked, perhaps that gentleman might be able to give it. With this he was obliged to be satisfied, for he could think of no one else to whom to apply.

Slowly he returned across the desolate moorlands, wondering many things over in his simple heart; he was deeply in debt, for the sickness and death of his two children and Margaret's long illness and need of nourishing food had cost him far more than he could afford. The money he hoped to get from his work at the wreck would not nearly suffice to pay all he owed; so with a heavy sigh, he determined to drive his cows to the next fair in the "town,"—for so the little hamlet, with its one wide dirty street, was designated by all the "countryside."

Then there was Agatha to think about. She, poor child, was evidently accustomed to better things than his rude cottage could offer. She tried in vain to eat the coarse oaten-cake, or the stirabout[1], of which Madge and Dennis made their hearty breakfasts and suppers; and at dinnertime she had stared with astonishment to see the huge pot of potatoes turned out into a basket, and each member of the family gathering round, taking the potatoes up in their fingers, stripping off their skins, and then eating them, with only a basin of milk and a little salt to make up the meal. So she had hitherto shared the luxuries which had been procured for Margaret—white bread and chicken broth—or a little rice cooked in milk. Her passionate distress had passed away, but often some little thing would open the fountain of her tears again, and she would sob bitterly and call for her nurse, "Mrs. Slade."

The name of the wrecked ship was the Queen of the Wave, and she was bound from the river St. Lawrence to Liverpool; she was not a passenger ship, but merely a trading vessel, with a cargo of timber and Indian corn; and how Agatha Buchanan came to be on board of her was a mystery to Antony. He questioned the child, but she knew very little, only that her "Uncle Frank had brought her and Catherine a long way in a carriage and had put them on board, telling her to be a good girl, and that Captain and Mrs. Royston would take care of her and take her to Grandmamma in England." She told further that her mamma was dead, and her father had gone away, though where he had gone she did not know: "Catherine knew;" and here the voice faltered, and Antony would ask no more.

On Sunday he led out his rough black pony to start for church; it was the first time he had been able to go since the

---

1   *porridge*

fever had come to his home, since one Sunday in June, when he and Margaret had returned to find John drooping and ailing with the approach of the sickness which had snatched him away. Those few short months, what changes they had made! Margaret could not bear him company now, but Agatha led her to the door to speak to him ere he set out. "I wish I was going with you," she said.

"You shall go with me yet, Madge dear, when ye have picked up a wee grain of strength; but I'm sorry to the heart to leave ye by yersel' with the childer, but—"

"You need not worrit about leaving me," said the blind woman, smiling, "this dear wee lassie is that careful of me, I shall want nothing; she is older, and graver like, than our Madgie, and minds me right well, that she does!"

Margaret's hand was resting on the child's shoulder, and at these words Agatha drew the fingers closer on her neck and laid her cheek upon them. "Yes," she said, "I will take care of her."

And Antony rode away, just as Madge and little Dennis came tumbling down the hillside, calling out "Father! Father! Mayn't we take Wavie down to the strand the day, while you are gone?"

"No; stay in the house and mind mother," was his reply. He had forbidden the children to take the little stranger on the strand, fearing that the tide might wash up some of the yet missing bodies of the companions of her voyage; and Madge and her brother, delighted with the society of their visitor, did not care to go without her.

"Why do they call me 'Wavie,'" asked Agatha of Margaret, "it is not my name."

"But your name is so hard, and so strange, Miss, our tongues can't get round it; and somehow wee Dennis called you Wavie, because you were washed ashore by the waves; you don't mind it, dear?"

"No; it is a pretty name, I think. You call me 'Wavie,' please, and not 'Miss'; nobody called me that until I was in this ship, and when you say it, I think I am there, and I can't help crying."

"Poor child; poor desolate bird!" Margaret's voice was full of sympathy, yet with ready tact she changed the direction of Agatha's thoughts, drying her tears by the never-failing expedient of claiming her help and attention.

The child forgot her grief as she guided the blind woman's steps to her chair beside the fire, and found a little stool for her feet, and a tiny shawl to keep the draught from her shoulders. She had never been accustomed to other children, and she felt shy of the shock-headed, bare-footed Madge and of the wondering-eyed Dennis. She would rather by far stay by Margaret's side than play about with them. And she felt a little afraid of Antony—a little conscience-stricken when she remembered how she had struggled in his arms and called him a "cruel man" and though his strong voice was always gentle when he spoke to her, yet she started at its sound and seemed uneasy in his presence. She was too young yet to appreciate the loving care he had shown her, though the time came when she did understand it thoroughly and returned it to him again with all the strength of her grateful heart.

The curate of Ardmore, who officiated at the little church that Sunday, was a stranger in the district, and indeed to Ireland. He was greatly astonished at Antony's communication, which he made as soon as the service was over.

"It is a sad story, a very sad story, my man," he said, "and not a creature was saved from the wreck except the little girl? Poor thing! But what can I do for you or for her?"

"It was only craving a bit of advice off yer riv'rence, that I was," replied Antony, a little hurt at the gentleman's tone; "your honor sees that there is no one to know anything about it in our place but the rector, and he's ill, more's the pity, so I made bold to spake to yersel'."

"Yes, yes; well, if I were you I should write to the owners of the Queen of the Wave, and see if they can tell you anything about the passengers. You can write?"

"It's but badly, sir, but I'd do my best, if I knew the direction where to send the letter."

"I'll try and get you the direction, or stay; I will write myself. Let me see! I cannot get an answer before Thursday or Friday. Can you come over to Ardmore on Friday, on the chance of an answer having arrived?"

"Well, ye see, sir, it's a long hit from here, and I live beyond this again—away at Glenderg; besides, I'm greatly thronged just now, what with one thing and another. Will your honor be here next Sunday?"

"It is most likely; indeed, almost certain, and then I will let you know."

Next Sunday came, but the clergyman had little news for Antony. He had heard from the shipowners, but they knew nothing of the little girl and her nurse who had taken passage in the Queen of the Wave. They had written to their agents in Canada for information on the subject, and in the meantime they gave the private addresses of the late Captain Royston and of Mr. Slade, the mate of the vessel; something, perhaps, might be traced through their means, they suggested.

"You must wait, you see," said the curate, as he finished reading this epistle to Antony. "I will write to these addresses, but I must say I think it very unlikely the people there will know anything of Agatha Buchanan. The Canada agents are our only chance, except that her friends, on their part, will be most eager to trace her and will be certain to make all possible enquiry. I should think there is every likelihood of her soon being taken off your hands, but at present, of course she is an expense and a burden. I will try to get up a little subscription for her present wants, but if nothing turns up concerning her belongings after a week or two, perhaps it might be better to send her to the workhouse."

Antony drew himself up to his full height, and his eye flashed.

"Thank yer riv'rence kindly for what ye have done, but there's no need to trouble yourself to get money for her; the wean has been heartily welcome to the wee bit and sup she has had, and even if her parents can't never be heard of, I'll keep her with me. It's not to the workhouse she shall go! Among thieves and swearers and such folk—and she come of gentle kin! If I saved her life, it was not to fling it into such a place as that!"

"Exactly as you like, my good man"; and the curate mounted his horse.

Antony watched him, uneasily. Had he been rude? He hastened to make excuse.

"I hope your honor will pardon me, if I spoke warm like; but 'tis as though God sent her to me instead of my own brave boys that lie over there in yon' corner, and I—"

He stopped short, for he perceived the gentleman had not heard him.

The feelings of the impulsive Irish peasantry are often misunderstood by the English visitors. And harsh, unjust judgments are often caused on both sides from this want of sympathy with each other. Antony was altogether unlike the hardheaded, practical Lancashire operatives, amongst whom the young curate had lived hitherto. He did not mean to be unkind. Indeed, he wished to serve the poor man who had spoken to him. But he was offended at the manner of the applicant, and he rode away, thinking how hasty the Irish nature was. "Who would fancy that decent-looking man was such a fire-eater?" he said to himself. "I only suggested the workhouse that he might be relieved of the charge of the child; and I'm sure she would be just as happy there, and quite as well taken care of as in his own rude hovel. I cannot understand why these people have such an absurd dread of going into the union! It isn't so in England; I suppose it arises from their abominable pride. Poor wretches! It is a marvel to me what they can find to be proud about."

The curate of Ardmore would have been shocked if one of his acquaintance had called him an unfeeling or a selfish man; yet it was clear that he had never learnt the full beauty of the Divine "charity" which "believeth all things, hopeth all things"—which will forge a link of sympathy between the highest and the humblest of the followers of Christ.

Chapter 6
AFTER TWO YEARS

If Antony was hurt at the curate's suggestion with regard to the workhouse, he heard it repeated often enough afterwards for him to grow accustomed to the idea; yet not for an instant did he meditate following the advice. He had written himself to the address given in the shipowner's letter, but he received no reply. Perhaps those to whom he had written had no information to give him; or, more likely, his handwriting, although it was his very best, and had given him infinite pains to perform, was not legible enough for post office officials. The clergyman had received a note from the Canadian agents, which he had forwarded to Antony; but they knew very little more than the people in Liverpool— nothing, indeed, which would serve as a clue; and they finished by recommending advertisements to be inserted in the Quebec and Montreal newspapers and paragraphs relating to the wreck of the Queen of the Wave to be sent to the English ones.

But this was beyond Antony's comprehension.

Newspapers, few and far between, had indeed found

their way to Glenderg, but their scope and circulation were
matters altogether too wide for his mental ken. God had sent
him the "wean," and he'd keep her, at least for the present.
The neighbors thought him mad to saddle himself with an
additional mouth to feed, an additional one to clothe and
care for, "now that times were so hard." They knew his cows
had been driven to the fair, and only one had come back, the
young heifer, the least valuable of the lot; and she had only
been spared because Margaret and "the wee lassie" could not
do without a drop of milk sometimes. "If all that owned her
were drowned," they urged, "or could not be heard of, why
should he keep her, who was nothing to her, but had done
a plenty for her already? Though, to be sure, poor child, she
was that pretty and had such coaxin' ways that it would be a
hard heart indeed that would not be good to her."

Margaret and Antony made no answer to this constant
show of interest in their affairs, except to say that Wavie was
as dear to them as if she had been kith and kin and that she
should stay as long as she chose, and be right welcome; God
bless her!

The probabilities seemed few in favor of the child being
claimed by her relatives. The account of the wreck of the
Queen of the Wave had appeared in the Londonderry papers
and had been copied, paragraph-wise, into some of the
London papers; and the notice concluded with the words,
"all on board perished." Total wrecks, even under such
awful circumstances, are of too common occurrence on the
western shores of Ireland to claim extraordinary attention,
unless they be emigrant ships or passenger steamers, when
the loss of life would be so fearful as to make all England
ring with the news. But in this case it was "merely" a barque
in the timber trade which had been shattered and broken
on the cruel rocks of Donegal, the captain and crew having
found the watery grave which is so close to every sailor's daily

life. Of the passengers, no one heard anything. Even Lloyd's agent, who came to the spot to look after the property and his colleague, "the Receiver of Wrecks," knew nothing of the existence of the little girl at the Creigans' cottage. The peasants of Glenderg had had such a share of plunder and rapine that they shrank away from the interrogations of the officials; they had their own reasons—and strong reasons too—for desiring that the hasty visit of the "strange gentlemen" should be as brief as it was possible for it to be.

Antony was not on the beach, but away at the fishing or working on his farm when they came, or he would gladly have tried to interest them in Agatha's story, or at least have begged them to give it what publicity they could, in the hope that it might eventually reach the ears of her distant kindred.

But this was not to be, at least not yet. For the present, the fisherman's home was to be her home—his rude lot hers. There was work for her to do at Glenderg—work which none could do as well as she, mere baby as she was in years, and unconscious of any power save the warm love of her heart.

So Wavie stayed. The weeks and months flew by, unmarked in their eventless round, until she had been an inmate of the cottage on the hillside for more than two years. The child was nine years old, and instead of the "grave white-faced bit of a thing," as the folks had called her, she was now as merry and nearly as rosy-cheeked as Madgie herself, though she had in no wise lost the easy gracefulness of manner and the simple dignity which distinguished her unmistakably from her companions. Her frock, of homespun woolen material, could not disguise the light, supple form; and her voice, while adopting something of the rich softness of the Irish "brogue" lost nothing of its own sweet intonation. Margaret fondly termed her "the blind woman's sunlight," and truly she was as the sunlight to her. It was a pretty sight to see them together, to watch the child striving by every means in her power to mitigate the affliction which weighed so heavily on Margaret's spirit. In the warm summertime Wavie would lead her down to the shore, finding her a comfortable seat on some dry rock, and would stand beside her and describe exactly how the sea looked: how far, far away it was blue, as blue as it could be; and then over towards Ennis Point it seemed purple, almost black, from the shadow of the great cloud which was rolling up from the south. And she would tell of the white seagulls swinging idly on the waves, not a stone's throw from the shore, and of the big grey crow stalking along by the water's edge, searching for dead fish or some jellyfish to carry off to his children in his nest on the old ruined Martello tower. Sometimes she would watch Antony's fishing boat, a mere speck on the surface of the sea, and she would tell Margaret exactly which way he was steering now or declare she was certain he had found something in that lobster trap, for he stayed such a time just in the very spot where he set it yesterday.

On other days they would go upon the moors, above the house, and Madge would bring heaps of wild flowers for Wavie to make garlands of; and she would sit at Margaret's feet, her fingers weaving the delicate blossoms, and her sweet voice chattering of their beauty to the sightless woman gaily and untiringly, for an hour together. Little Dennis would break off huge fronds of the royal fern and bring them, twice as tall as himself they were, for his mother's admiration; and when both Madge and Dennis were weary of roaming about, they would come and throw themselves down on the springy heather, while Wavie sang to them songs that she had learned in the distant land from which she had come, and which, from constant practice, she had never forgotten. It was small marvel that Margaret called her "Sunshine."

Then in the summertime there was the kelp burning
to see to, and this was prime fun for the children! On
some parts of the western coast of Ireland, they burn
large quantities of this "kelp," or barilla, as it is otherwise
termed; and Wavie and Madge, and even little Dennis,
helped Antony dry the seaweed in the blazing sun, tossing
and spreading it as if it had been hay. Then there was
the building of it into little stacks, "the father," as they
all three called him, doing the building part, and the
children tottering along with huge armsful of the dry,
crisp stuff. And when many cocks, or stacks, stood there
on the sandbanks in goodly array, the kiln was made—a
shallow trench about six or seven feet long and one or two
feet wide. Here a fire was kindled, and when it had burnt
up clear and bright, the dry seaweed was thrown on, to
crackle and burn as fast as might be. How it did burn, to
be sure! And how it did smoke! Thick clouds of smoke, as
white as milk, and so thick that the children could not see
their father if the column rolled between, even though he
might not be two yards away from them. But this dense
smoke column hung together marvellously. Too heavy to
mix readily with the atmosphere, it swept off before the
faint breeze, creeping along the ground, and often not
finally dispersing until it had kept its line unbroken for
more than a mile. Carefully to windward Antony took his
stand, watching for the tongues of scarlet flame to force
themselves through; and when they came, he would fling
on more seaweed, and more and more, until all their sea
harvest was consumed. Then Paddy and Hugh O'Donnel,
and some other of the neighbors, would gather round
with iron rods and beat and pound the red-hot lava-like
stuff which remained in the kiln; until, gradually cooling,
it stuck together, and they formed it into large blocks of
bluish-grey substance, into kelp—in fact, the kelp which

was to be shipped to Glasgow, to help to make iodine, and soap, and plenty of other useful things, and to bring many shillings to reward Antony and his children for their busy summer's work.

But it could not be always summertime; and the children could not always run like wild colts about the rocks and shores of Glenderg. Long days of gloom came, when the wind mourned and wailed round the cottage; and heavy splashes of rain or hail were dashed against the tiny panes of glass which formed its windows; and strong gusts of wind came rushing from off the sea, or from the mountain glens towards the north, so fierce and so strong that they lifted bits of thatch and whirled them away in spite of the strong straw ropes, and sundry stones, and planks which had been laid on the roof to keep it down.

Wavie did not like the wintertime: she was not so strong as her little companions, and she could not brave the rain and blasts as they could. The cruel cold made her cough and gave her a pain in her chest; so she generally kept close by the turf fire, her head on Margaret's knee, watching the glittering knitting needles flashing in the light, as the long warm stocking grew rapidly beneath the blind woman's dexterous fingers.

Nelly Brennan, a "widow woman" living hard by, came every day to "rid up a bit"; she did the housework which was too heavy for the children to manage; and, in return, Antony "labored her potato field" for her, and gave mountain grazing to her one cow, and did sundry other neighborly acts for her. Nelly and her son Owen needed a strong arm to thresh their small crop of oats and to dig and delve their scattered patches of fields—for Owen was only a lad, too young to undertake much as yet, though he exerted himself manfully to supply his dead father's place. The Creigans needed a woman's homely hand to do

what Margaret's blindness rendered it impossible for her
to perform. And thus each household was benefitted and
helped by the law of kindness.

Wavie's memories of her Canadian life did not wax
dim. She used to talk to Margaret for hours about her
uncle's house across the sea, about his children, and
about his beautiful garden. And she would tell Madge
and Owen Brennan of the woods, the grand somber pine
forests, where the trees stood in neverending rows, lifting
their dark tops high against the sky. She would tell about
the heavy snow lying feet deep all around, covering up
everything except the giant trees, which stood unchanged,
knee-deep as it were, in the powdery, glittering snow. She
would tell of the summertime, when she and her cousins
would ramble away to seek for squirrels in those same
woods, when the hot sunshine came bathing all the world
and scorching everything around; yet there, beneath the
pines, the shades lay cool and soft, and the green light fell
lovingly upon the moss.

Madge and Owen would listen and wonder: wonder
how those forests must really appear—wonder how trees
could grow so many and so high. The only trees they had
ever seen on their bare, brown moorlands were the three
mountain ashes which grew at the foot of the cliff at Lough
Illion, the three which were known for miles round as the
"fairy rowan trees, beneath Lough Illion spink[1]."

But though she talked often of her former life, Wavie
was very happy at Glenderg, notwithstanding her changed
position—happy in her own sweet, thoughtful way. She was
specially fond of reaching down Antony's big Bible and
reading aloud to Margaret from its sacred pages. In the
stormy days when the cold kept her indoors, and the wind
came shrieking round the cottage, the fair-haired child

---

1   cliff

would read on and on, placing little paper markers at the chapters which seemed to her simple mind the most to be admired, because they were the clearest to be understood. Margaret would listen as she knitted, and Nelly Brennan would stay awhile sometimes after her work was done, to hear the beautiful words; and her son Owen would hush his boyish play while Wavie read about that dreadful storm at sea, when the ship was well nigh lost; when all her crew and passengers were so sorely frightened—all but the holy man of God, the brave Apostle Paul. Nelly would ask to hear again of the broken-hearted widow of Nain, how she followed the corpse of her only son towards the grave, and how her mourning was turned into joy by the words of the blessed Lord Jesus as he met the funeral at the gate of the city.

When Antony came home in the evening, he would inquire what they had been reading that day; and then they would talk about it all, until the holy men of olden time became familiar as living personages to them. Their voices grew reverent and solemn as they spoke of the Lord and His gentle sorrowful human life amongst the children of men.

There was poverty and there was ignorance in the Creigans' cottage, but there were also heavenly riches and truest wisdom: the riches "which moth and rust cannot corrupt" and the wisdom which is "more precious than rubies." And from that humble home the gospel light shone out, bright and clear into the thick darkness around.

Nelly and her son never imagined that their priest would have angrily forbidden them to listen to the words of the Book that they found so beautiful and so true. Controversy had never been stirred up at Glenderg: Protestantism and Popery alike had lain quietly asleep;

but the wakening time was come, and deep into many a heart sank the words of Antony's Bible; and many a mind pondered on the brightness which kept Margaret's smile serene in spite of her affliction, which kept Antony's rough tones hearty and blithe when money was scarce and times were hard, and which shone on Agatha Buchanan's face—stranger and waif, as she was—until it seemed to them as the face of an angel.

Chapter 7
A Burden or a Blessing

The summertime had come again, but with it came serious cause for anxiety. The people looked grave as they went into the fields to dig their meals of the early potatoes; they sighed as they saw the sere tops, showing the fatal yellow hue, which told only too surely of the disease which was at their roots. The crop was bad. It sounds but a little thing to say, but it meant terrible things to the poor creatures who mournfully repeated the words to each other: it meant debt and a struggle with dire distress—it meant empty cow houses and land lying waste for lack of seed to sow it with; it meant even a worse thing than all these—hunger itself!

How little many of us think of the true meaning of the words we use when we pray the Lord to "succor, help, and comfort all that are in necessity and tribulation." It may be that the world smiles on us and that in silken robe or finest broadcloth we pray for the poor and needy. Or it may be that we are entirely wrapped up in our own concerns, our own sorrows, joys, plans, anxieties: so entirely absorbed by ourselves as to have no time to realize what we utter, when we pray with our lips—as we hold ourselves bounden to do—

for all those who are in sorrow, need, or sickness, for those
who are desolate and afflicted. Certain it is, that the mass
of human suffering and human woe is little regarded by the
favored children of wealth and luxury. Money they give, freely
and generously sometimes, and pity also, when they see some
heart-rending spectacle of misery or hear some dismal tale of
the distress that is so near to them; but Sympathy—the sacred
fellow-feeling with another, not merely for him—this is rare
indeed!

In all the wide earth, there seemed no one to know or
to heed the trouble that had come upon Glenderg. The
landowner was a great English lord, too busy with his own
affairs to think of his barren Irish acres, or the peasantry who
paid him rent for them. He was not a hard man; his agent
had orders to keep things as they were: not to raise the rent
roll or to be too severe on the tenantry. And so he considered
his duty was accomplished, that neither God nor man had
reason to lay the sin of oppression or cruelty at his door.

The people did not complain. As it had been in their
fathers' time, so it was in theirs; they did not complain, but
their crop had failed; they must suffer in silence and bear
their sufferings as best they could!

"Madge," said Antony one day, as he stood leaning against
the cottage door, "Madge, the praties won't last us through
October. I've been thinking of going to Derry for a load or
two of Indian meal; we shall get it a power cheaper there nor
here!"

"But there is the fetching of it nigh on forty mile," she
responded, "and there is what is worse again nor the fetching,
and that is the paying for it; how could ever we raise money
enough to pay for one sack, let alone two?"

"There is the horse, Madge."

"Oh, Anton, that should be the last thing to go—think of

all the leagh[1] you draw up from the strand with the poor beast; and isn't drawing home Michael Moore's turf the only way ye can pay off the claim he has on us for last winter's meal? If ye sell the horse we're done entirely."

"The creatur' must go some time or other," he said, with a sigh, "and better go first when we can get food by the ready money, than last, when it will only pay off a share of our debt. And besides, it's Michael Moore hisself that offers me whole nine poun' for him, after deducting the trifle I owe him still; and he also says I may bring the meal from Derry with the beast, if I'm so minded, he giving me the nine poun' in my hand. It's a rare offer, Madge, but he's that keen for the horse that I believe he'd give me ten poun' rather than not have him."

"Ay," said Margaret, a little proudly, "there is not the likes of our pony in all the country round; that's well known, and it's the more sorry I am to part with him."

"There is the childer to think on before the horse. Five mouths to feed, woman dear! They'll crave a plenty."

"Father," said a little voice at his elbow.

Antony started as he saw Wavie standing beside him.

"I've been sitting on the rock yonder," she said, "and I have heard what you have been talking about. I heard, too, something which Michael's wife said to Nelly Brennan yesterday; she said, father, that it was hard on you to have to feed and clothe me, who am none of your own children, but a stranger from foreign lands; and she said it was only foolishness of you to be giving me shoes and stockings and giving in to my grand notions, putting me above your own children, who went about barefoot weekdays and Sundays; and she said no one would thank you for it—that you were robbing Mammy here, and Madge, and Dennis, and may be nourishing a serpent in your bosom the whole time. I remember just the very words," added the poor child, in a shaking voice, "for they sank right

---

1   *seaweed*

into my heart; and I have been so sorry, so sorry that I have
been a burden to you."

"You have not been a burden to us, but just the light of
the house," burst in Antony's indignant voice, while Margaret
throwing down her knitting, came to place her arms round the
child, to soothe her sobs with her motherly caresses.

"It was a sin and a shame to speak such words as them!"
went on Antony. "I'll step down to Michael's this minute,
and—"

"No, you won't either," said Margaret, "no good would
come of it, and Wavie won't mind about it when she hears
us say it's all untrue; sure ye won't, darlin'? Why what would
we have done without ye, dear? Who would lead me up and
down? Who would mind the weans for me? Who would get
Antony's dinner, many's the day? I've always said that when the
Lord took from me the sight of my eyes, He sent you to me to
be the glint of sunshine in my poor dark home. Child! Child!
Sure and ye believe it?"

Held tight in those loving arms, and with Antony's rough
hand smoothing down her hair, how could she refuse to
believe it? How could she doubt but that she was as welcome,
nay, as treasured as their own child could ever be.

"Now, don't ye be listening if ye hear them sort of things
again," said Antony, "and don't ye be frettin' because times will
be hard this year: we're in God's hands, ye must remember, and
we'll weather the storm this time. Who knows but that you
yersel' may bring good fortune to us all yet! When it turns out
that you're some grand lady with hundreds of poun's of your
own, we'll be axing ye to do great things for us, every one, that's
what we will! Won't we, Madge?"

So Wavie smiled through her tears.

She had been so unhappy in her grave childish fashion
that the kind cheery words of her foster parents seemed
like a rush of sunlight to her. "If I was indeed a grand

lady," she replied, "you would have no time to ask me for anything, for I would buy you a new coat and ever so many cows. And mother should have a big chair, with rockers and cushions to it, like uncle's chairs in Canada, and we would have a carriage to ride to church—oh, I forgot," the child said, suddenly interrupting herself, "I quite forgot about the horse. Oh, are you really going to sell him to Michael Moore?"

"Yes, dear. And we'll buy such a store of meal with the money! And, maybe, something else besides."

She stood silently looking through the doorway; and Antony, taking his hat from the table, left the cottage; then Wavie turned to Margaret:

"I have eaten a great deal of meal and many, many potatoes since you saved me from the sea," she said; "if it had not been for me, perhaps—"

"Wavie, mavourneen, would ye wish to bring sorrow to Antony's heart? And he loving ye as if ye were his own flesh and blood, just? If ye would be vexing him, and vexing me, talk like that again; but if it's pleasing us you'd be, forget all them words ye heard and only remember that I thank the Lord each night for the sending of ye here."

"Do you really never feel sorry, never? Never?"

"Yes, dear; sometimes when I think that there may be those who love you, and mourn for the loss of you, only then am I sorry, and only for them; so ye may—"

"Oh, mother! What is that?"

There was a crash heard and a smothered shout; the sound came through the open door, startling them both. The blind woman wrung her hands.

"It was Antony that called. Oh, Wavie, he is hurt! He is kilt!"

"What's to hurt him, mother? Stay here," and Wavie led her to the great rock beside the door. "Stay here, and I will

run and see. I'll be back in no time," and off she flew, almost
as swiftly as the white gulls which were wheeling round the
cliffs of Ennis Head.

Straight down from the cottage door, the footpath went
between masses of grey granite, beside the small plots of
cultivated land, which had been reclaimed from the bog,
where the oats were standing high, and the diseased potatoes
showed their yellow withered foliage. Some three hundred
yards down this pathway, about halfway to the shore, stood
a cottage which had been empty since the terrible famine
time of 1846. Its inmates had all been swept away, and there
had been found no tenants for it since; therefore the fields
had been annexed to Antony's farm, and he had used the
half-ruined cabin as a shelter for his cows or a storehouse for
such possessions as were too bulky or too worthless to be
located in his own house.

Down the footpath Wavie ran, towards the ruined
cottage; it was the only direction from which the sound
which had so startled them could have come, for behind
their house rose the high granite cliffs, and above them
again stretched out the broad moorlands, where one
rarely met a living thing, save the timid grouse, and hares,
crouching among the heather. The pathway turned and
twisted among the stones and beside the potato ridges; but
no impediments delayed Wavie's little feet. She reached the
cabin door; it stood wide open, but the light penetrated
only a little way into the dark interior, and the small
window had long been stuffed up with straw to keep out
wind and rain. She could see nothing unusual, and she was
about to hasten onwards, when a sound like a smothered
groan caught her attention.

"Oh, father! Father!" she called, "where are you? Are you
hurt? Father!"

But there was no reply, and Wavie, with a beating heart,

passed on through the broken door, groping her way through
the darkness. She gained the center of the floor and stopped,
bewildered, in an agony of wondering fear. Again came the
smothered groan. And now, her eyes getting accustomed to
the gloom, she perceived on one side what seemed to her
like the figure of a man lying upon a pile of wood. In one
instant she was beside it. It was indeed Antony, and beside
him lay broken planks and sticks heaped around; while right
across his chest rested a huge beam of wood, crushing his life
out with its cruel weight. The child, with a loud cry, flung
herself on her knees, and pushed against it with all her might,
sobbing out his name, and imploring him to speak to her.
But Antony could not hear her; her voice was for once calling
to him in vain, and he lay there before her as insensible and
helpless as she herself had lain when he had found her on the
shore that terrible day, more than two years ago.

Chapter 8
THE FALLEN BEAM

Wavie pushed with all her strength against the great beam, but the foam flakes might as soon hope to move the boulders on Glenderg strand, as she to lift that big brown plank with her tiny white hands. She saw presently how useless her efforts were, and she knelt there beside Antony in blank despair. Her forehead rested against his arms, and her fingers clasped his hand, while in her heart was the thought which had almost benumbed her with its agony—"He is dead! He is dead!" But he was not dead, for again came the faint groan, fainter than ever, now, yet enough to rouse Wavie to instant action. If she was powerless to help him, she must seek someone who could. She sprang to her feet and ran out of the cabin, not up the hill—there was no one but Margaret in the cottage, and what could she do?—but down towards the shore to seek aid there from such of the neighbors as might happen to be at hand. Three or four men were standing at the turn of the road; her breathless words sent them hurrying towards the ruin, far too fast for her to keep pace with them. The excitement and exertion she had gone through began to tell on her frail strength, and she leant against the stone wall faint and white. Her brain seemed in a whirl; she could not think; she could not even pray.

"Wavie, Wavie, what is the matter? What ails you?" she lifted her head wearily. Little Madge was standing close beside her, looking into her face with wondering eyes, while a step or two behind came Owen Brennan, the widow's son; Dennis was seated astride on his shoulders, carrying a basket of limpets and periwinkles, which the three children had collected on the rocks.

Owen set Dennis, basket and all, safely on the ground, and then he too repeated Madge's question: "What ails you, Wavie, ahaska?"

The sympathy in his voice quite broke her down, and her sobs came fast as she answered:

"The father is killed—crushed to death, Owen; he was moving about some things in the old house, and the beam gave way and struck him down. It is lying right on him now, across his breast; and I could not move it, I could not!—Oh, Owen!"

"Have you sent nobody? I will go," and he was springing away, when her agonized voice called him back.

"John, and Patrick, and James Duffy are gone; oh, Owen, stay a minute, and let me go with you! There is mother to be told, what am I to say to her? She will die too." And again the sobs came thick and fast. And Madge cried aloud, half in terror, and half because Wavie did, while Dennis looked from her face to his shellfish, and back again to her face in the utmost bewilderment.

Owen came close up to her and placed his strong arm in its tattered jacket sleeve around the sobbing child.

"Wavie, dear, don't take on so. Don't ye mind what ye read to us out of the big book last Monday night, about all things joining together for good to them such as love the Lord? Sure,

Antony and Margaret and you, Wavie, love Him, so ye'll find
that 'tis not death, but some good thing which this day will
bring to ye. Ye can't heed me now, darlin', your heart is that
full! But ye'll mind of it again when the sorrow clears off a
bit. Lean hard on my shoulder, dear, and we'll be up at your
house in no time."

"Hullo, Madge! And you Dennis, don't you ones be
running on in front; just go down to the shore, and tell my
mother to come up to Antony's, right away; and you too can
come up with her. Now, Wavie!"

And so the barefooted peasant boy half carried her along
the rude pathway, speaking strong cheery words as they went,
words which were echoes of those he had caught from her
lips during the hours he had listened to her reading aloud
from the pages of Antony's Bible.

Those Bible words had fallen on good ground when they
entered Owen's heart. They did not come to him as an oft
told tale heard from earliest childhood or as a lesson to be
learnt laboriously and drearily; but they came to him as
something new, and strange, and beautiful: filling his soul
with reverence and love. The simple boy, whose whole range
of human knowledge did not extend beyond the mountains
which shut off Glenderg from the rest of the world with
its huge stony barrier—he, like Antony Creigan, realized
the Divine "Good news," the truths of this Gospel, with
an intensity of faith, which thousands of earth's wise and
wealthy ones would give all their wisdom and all their wealth
to possess. It was of such of those humble ones that our
Saviour spoke when he said: "I thank Thee, O Father, Lord of
heaven and earth, because Thou hast hid these things from
the wise and prudent, and hast revealed them unto babes:
even so, Father, for so it seemed good in Thy sight!"

As the children went up the hill, they saw the group of
men bearing Antony's unconscious form from the ruined

cottage to his home. With the claim on her energy, new life seemed to dart into Wavie's exhausted frame. She took her hand from Owen's shoulder.

"I must go and tell mother," she said, "and, oh, Owen! We have never sent any one for the doctor; will you go?"

"Troth and will I; I will take the horse beast, and it won't be long before Dr. Doran is here, if he's to be found at all, at all. But yourself, Wavie? Sure you won't go for to take on so again? You will just be quiet and patient like, and let mother do everything; see yonder she comes."

"Yes, yes; but go, Owen, go! And ride fast!" she urged, feverishly; and then, not noticing the doubtful lingering look on his anxious face, she broke from him and darted up towards the house, passing with averted eyes the men who silently bore the senseless, nerveless form of him who had trodden that very path not half an hour ago, in the full strength and prime of manhood. Wavie could not look on his face; she felt instinctively that had she done so the deadly faintness which had overcome her on the shore would return to her again, then who was to tell Margaret?

On she ran, until she saw the figure of the blind woman standing beside the great grey stone at her cabin door, waiting, still waiting for the word Wavie had promised to bring. Ah, what terrible news it was!

"Mother," said the child, with panting breath, "dear mother, father is hurt; it was a beam in the old house that did it. Oh, mother, speak to me! Don't look like that!"

"Is he dead?" and Margaret's voice came hollow and hoarse from between her white, drawn lips.

"No, no! I think not; I am sure not; they are bringing him up; they are quite near; don't you hear their tread? We shall soon know where he is hurt; oh, no, he is not killed; he is not—"

"Child, child, don't tell me lies! He is killed; I know it!

Antony, Antony!" and she burst out into the loud storm of
distress which only those who have witnessed it in an Irish
nature can form any idea of. She followed them as they
carried her husband over the threshold, and then flinging
herself on the floor beside the bed, she wept and moaned and
tore her long dark hair in a paroxysm of despair and grief.
The neighbors stood by with pitying words and looks, but
they did not attempt to comfort her.

"It's no wonder she's fairly distraught; the creature!" said
Nelly Brennan, who had come in with Madge and Dennis.
"Just let her greet away; it will ease the sore heart of her."

But Wavie had never seen or heard such violent sorrow
before. She came close to Margaret, patting her with her little
hands and imploring her to be calm. But Margaret could not
be calm. She dashed away the children who came clinging
to her side; she turned away from Wavie passionately, even
roughly; she refused to be comforted. Owen had entreated
his little companion to be "quiet and patient." He would not
have thought the words necessary could he have seen her
now. It was she who with unchildlike thoughtfulness hung
on a kettle that the doctor might find boiling water when he
came, in case he might need it. It was she who edged her way
in through the people gathered round the bed and cut off the
thick matted hair through which the blood was slowly oozing,
and then she bound strips of her own little frock across her
foster father's brow, to stanch as well as she could that purple
stream. Many hands would have helped her, had they only
known how; but they were so busy in talking and wondering
over the sad occurrence that they seemed to have forgotten
that there was work to do, and that they might have helped to
do it. But Wavie moved about with her gentle steps, soothing
the frightened children, trying vainly to quiet Margaret's
stormy grief, and ever and anon looking out along the road
for the first glimpse of Owen, with the doctor.

She saw them at last—at last! The hours had seemed as years to her; for might not this long delay cost her foster father his life?

"Here comes Dr. Doran," said Pat Boner; "now we shall know if the breath is in him at all. It's my belief it's clean gone, entirely; but I'll be able to say for certain the moment the doctor begins handling of him. It is altogether wonderful to see our doctor working with what he calls his 'cases,'— meaning folks as is ill or hurt anyways—altogether wonderful! I admire to see him."

But Dr. Doran had no mind to give Patrick any scope for his admiration or wonderment in the present instance. He entered the cottage and marched straight up to the bed in the outer room, on which Antony was lying; he gave one look at his corpse-like face, and then turned round to the people standing by.

"I say, my friends,"—he began in a business-like tone—"if there is any chance for Antony Creigan's life, he must have air, and I must have light and silence. So the best thing you can all do is to clear the house at once. I will look in at Boner's cottage as I ride away and tell you all my opinion of him; but now, every creature leave this place immediately, except you, Nelly; you may stay to help me, as I see Margaret is fit for nothing."

He went up to the poor distracted wife: "Margaret, won't you go down with the children to some neighbor's? I must have silence here!"

Wavie touched his arm. "Oh, sir, please let me stay." The blind woman had arisen at the doctor's words, but the nervous excitement to which she had given way, and the very violence of her grief proved too much for her. She staggered, and with one long-drawn sigh fell in a dead faint at Wavie's feet.

"Ah, poor thing!" said the compassionate doctor; "it is the

best thing that could happen to her. Lay her head down, my little girl, and leave her alone, and then run away with all the others, and let me set to work."

"Oh, sir," pleaded Wavie again, "do please let me stay." Dr. Doran looked keenly at the little fair face, so childlike, and yet so womanly in its intensity of expression. "Yes," said he, "you may stay, and what is more, you can help me." So Wavie stayed.

Chapter 9
The Border Land

It seemed truly as if sorrow and trial had reached their extremest limits in Antony's cottage. He did not die, but he lay for many days without power to move hand or foot, speechless and senseless, tended by Nelly Brennan and Wavie. Kind Dr. Doran rode daily down the rugged Glenderg road: he was resolved his patient should not suffer from the lack of any aid or skill that he could supply. Antony Creigan had long been a favorite of his: he had noticed his manly resignation by the deathbeds of his boys; he had sympathized in his anguish when he knew that his wife must be blind; he had heard of the ready welcome he had given to the little stranger, cast by the storm upon his hands, and how he refused for her to be sent to the workhouse, though times were hard and the crop was bad. Dr. Doran was a busy man. He was the parish doctor for a large tract of mountainous country, and his daily rides were rough and far; yet he always managed to find time for a cheering word when he saw such was required. He was not rich; the people were very poor, and paying patients were rare indeed; yet many a shilling found its way from his pockets into the hands of the needy and destitute. Truly, it was a small wonder Dr. Doran was beloved.

Antony was dreadfully hurt. The falling beam had almost crushed his life out; the doctor feared he never could be a strong man again, even if he recovered sufficiently to rise from his sick bed. No more long days' work for Antony—other hands must labor in his fields now. Other arms must send his boat cutting through the sea, urged by the powerful sweep of the oars. Others must bring his heavy loads of seaweed on their backs up the steep road from the shore. And who could do all this? How could he afford to pay for labor? He who had seemed in distress enough to give serious cause for anxious thought before this last blow came! The doctor knew all this, and so did Margaret; but the children talked happily of the time when "father would be well again." As for Antony himself, no one knew what he thought of, or whether he thought at all. When the first days of insensibility and stupor had passed away, other days succeeded scarcely less silent, scarcely less deathlike. He would lie for hours in the dim light, with closed eyes and contracted brow; and they only knew he was not sleeping by seeing his eyes unclose and the pale lips smile at them when they approached his bed.

It was a terrible time for Margaret. The passionate first burst of her sorrow had left her almost in despair. Her faith was not so real, nor so perfect, as that of her husband; and it lacked the simple trustfulness of Wavie and Owen's. She hardly listened now when Wavie, according to her old custom, reached down the big Bible and read aloud some of the favorite pages where she and Antony had placed long golden straws to mark the places where the most beautiful stories, or the most loved texts, were to be found. Margaret's soul was dark and almost hopeless. What was the trial of her blindness in comparison to this? God had laid His hand too heavily on her, she thought; how could she help but rebel?

Like Jonah, in her secret heart she felt that she "did well to be
angry."

One day, as the afternoon was merging into evening,
Margaret sat on her doorstep, knitting. The children had
gone down to the rocks to gather shellfish during the ebb
tide. Dr. Doran had paid his visit, and Nelly Brennan had
gone to her own cottage for awhile. Antony was lying quiet,
as usual, his labored breathing coming painfully from his
bruised chest and sounding distressingly loud in the hush
of the summer afternoon. Dark, gloomy thoughts filled the
blind woman's heart; she knitted on rapidly, more from habit
than from any real reason; though, indeed, there was need
enough for all the pennies her needles could earn.

"Madge, woman!"

The words were spoken in a strange, choking kind of
whisper, but they rang clear as a bell on the blind woman's
ears. She rose and knelt beside the bed.

"I am here, Antony."

"Give over your hand to me, wife, and hold me tight,
tight! I have come back to ye, but I've been far."

She thought he was wandering and bade him "hush."

"I've been far," he repeated, "even to the Valley of the
Shadow of Death, and just one step beyond me was the river,
that river the hymn speaks about; what is it? I can't mind the
words."

"I don't know, Antony."

"Ah, well; it does not matter: I have been in the valley that
leads to the river; I looked across it, and I could see a great
light shining round the country on the other shore; but the
valley where I have been was very dark at first, and I could
hardly bear the sharp pain and the black darkness. But after
a while I saw, right fornenst me, the face of the Lord leaning
down towards me through the clouds; and He smiled and
said, 'Not yet; you must turn back again: you cannot cross

the river now; but fear not; for, lo, I am with you always, even
unto the end of the world.' And so, as I was lying there I saw
ye all like in a dream; and now I know as I am to stay with ye,
yet awhile."

Margaret listened to him wonderingly, and then her
thoughts flew onward to the future she dreaded, with its long
years of want and care, and the bitter words came to her lips,
she knew not how:

"Maybe it's the worse for ye to come back to us; there's
little rest or joy that I can see this side of the grave."

But Antony's mind was still dwelling on the beauty of the
dream or vision that had been sent to comfort him in his sore
pain and need, and he did not catch the meaning of his wife's
words, though he heard their sound.

"Rest, and joy, is it? Ay, I heard the child reading about it
last night: 'There remaineth therefore a rest for the people of
God.'"

He was silent. The evening wind came whispering round
the hill; the long roll of the Atlantic broke softly on the
low-water mark; the bees were busy with the heather and
thyme, on their last journey that day, for the sun was pouring
its sunset flood of crimson light upon the sea; the voices
of the children came faintly from the shore. "Rest!" The
echo of the word sank deep into Margaret's soul. "There
remaineth therefore a rest for the people of God." And when
the tempter whispered the ready response, "But such Rest is
only for God's people, and you have hardly been acting as
such," amid a flood of tears came the blessed words to her
memory—"Him that cometh unto Me, I will in no wise cast
out."

With every one of those tears the ice of distrust and
rebellion seemed melting away from Margaret's heart. How
faithless she had been! How wicked and weak! In the glorious
Book which had been such a teacher, such a comforter in the

Creigans' home, were the words: "Like as a father pitieth his children, so the Lord pitieth them that fear Him." And that Divine pity came now to her. Sin was not to have undisputed dominion over her; for it is not the will of our Father in Heaven that one of His children should perish.

Long she knelt there. By Antony's hushed and regular breathing, the blind wife knew that he slept. For the first time since that terrible day, words of prayer and thankfulness came from her lips. She could come to the mercy seat now—come to implore the pardon she needed so sorely; and she could return an offering of praise now, praise for her husband's life, given back from the jaws of the grave, and praise for the blessed knowledge that the Lord Jesus was her Saviour and her Friend.

She felt she could trust Him now for the future and leave all things in His hands. He fed the birds that hung their nests on the face of the bare, cold cliff; He sent sunshine and rain to the flowers that covered the moors with their carpet of beauty; she knew He reckoned her little household—Antony, the children, and herself—as of far greater value than the birds and the flowers. He would send them such things as He knew they really needed, sorrow and trial, maybe; but sorrow and trial would soon be forgotten in the light of His smile; and whatever might come, did not there remain "a Rest for the people of God"?

Chapter 10
WAVIE'S PLANS

The children came up from the shore in high glee. Wavie and Dennis carried baskets filled with periwinkles and limpets and the long brown fronds of the dulse, or "delisk," as the people of Donegal term their favorite edible seaweed. But little Madge's basket contained a yet greater treasure: even two great lobsters, who lay whisking their long horns in energetic disapproval of their unexpected captivity.

"Oh, mammy," said Dennis, "they are so big, I wish you could feel them! Just try; I'll guide yer hand and watch they don't nip hold on ye."

But Margaret wisely declined trusting her fingers within reach of the powerful claws, at any rate under Dennis' auspices.

"We got them in a hole at the very end of Carickarn," said Madge, eagerly; "we should never have got them by oursel's; but Owen, he catched them just on the backs and jerked them right out; and one of them—that one, the biggest of the two—fell just at Wavie's feet, and she gave such a start that she slipped and fell backward into a pool; oh, it was such fun!"

"Mavourneen, did ye hurt yersel'? You're wet!"

"Salt water never hurts anybody, mother dear! At least so you often tell us."

"Ay, but you are not so strong as the likes of us; you must be careful down on them sluthery rocks, Wavie. And now come into the house, and boil some of them winkles for supper—and one of the lobsters, too, if ye like."

"Both, both of them! Mammy," urged Dennis, "let's have a bonnie feast the night."

"They're big ones, ye say? What would ye think childer, of giving the biggest to the doctor tomorrow? He's ever so kind and good to us, and it's just nothing we can do to show we are thankful to him. He'd like one of the beasts, I know, for the quality count a great deal on lobsters."

So the finest was set aside for the doctor, even little Dennis declaring "it wasn't begrudging it to him he'd be, for didn't he give him a bright copper penny only yesterday?"

Dr. Doran was greatly pleased with the gift. "It's a pleasure to carry it," he said to Margaret, as she, with the true courtesy of the Irish, was profusely apologizing for not being able to send it to his house for him, as Wavie could not walk so far, and the little ones were too small to venture on the long journey.

"Do you often get these things?" asked the gentleman; "if so, your children might earn some money, if you could only get them conveyed to Miramore. They would sell rapidly there."

"Yes, in troth would they," replied Nelly Brennan, who was standing by, "and so they would in Dublin!—meaning no offense to yer honor by saying the same."

"You think it as likely to be able to send them to Dublin as to Miramore, Nelly? But I'm not so sure that you're right. Old Neil often goes round Forman Head with his boatload of kelp at this season of the year. Don't you know he quarrelled

with Manus Boyle long ago? So as nobody buys kelp here
excepting Manus, Neil is obliged to take his all the way to
Miramore. I dare say he would give the children a passage for
their lobsters."

Wavie listened with sparkling eyes. She had long puzzled
over in her little brain possible ways and means of helping
the generous friends who had been so good to her; but
hitherto she had puzzled in vain. There seemed to be nothing
a child, like her, could accomplish. She could not even do
the embroidery, which so many of the Glenderg lasses were
expert in. She had often watched their busy fingers over their
long "webs of sprigging," as they called the yards of trimming
which they made of sewed-muslin work; and as she watched
them, she longed that she too could earn money; but she was
so unknowledgeable, she sadly thought, there seemed nothing
she could do. The pony had been led away from Antony's
fields to those of Michael Moore, and the money which his
sale had brought was now supplying the household with food,
for the wretched potato crop was already gone. But Wavie
remembered the conversation she, Antony, and Margaret
had had the very morning of the accident: she knew the nine
pounds would not last very long; and what were they to look
to then? Even with her hopeful and ignorant view of the case,
she knew it must be many months before her foster father
could again earn anything himself. If she could only do some
little thing to help, instead of being merely an extra expense
and burden!

Dr. Doran's words were as a revelation to her. She followed
him as he went to the door to mount his horse.

"Please, sir, is there anything else that we children could
gather on the shore which the gentlefolks at Miramore would
buy? For it is not often we can catch lobsters like this,"—
touching the basket which hung upon his arm,—"and I do so
much want to earn money."

The doctor smiled down at the little maiden, looking imploringly and shyly at him through the tresses of the bright fair hair, which the wind was tossing across her eyes. "You want to earn money, my dear? Well, it is not a particularly easy thing to do in these parts, but you are quite right to try. Gather some winkles, and cockles, and mussels by the next time Neil's boat crosses to Miramore. I fear you won't get very much for them, but every little helps, you know; and if you can get a lobster or two, why so much the better."

Dr. Doran was far too delicate to offer money in return for the gift he was carrying away with him. He well knew nothing would have hurt the giver's feelings more than so doing; but he was resolved to repay them amply, nevertheless. An idea struck him at that moment.

"Do you know what carageen is?" he asked.

"No, sir."

"Owen can show you, if you ask him; he got me some once; it is a short, black kind of seaweed which grows on the rock at Ennis Point; and black as it is, you must bleach it until it is quite white. Then let it lie in the sun until it is thoroughly dry and crisp. I shall be over here constantly for a long time, and I will see how it is getting on; and when it is quite white, and dry enough, I will give you money for it, because it is exceedingly useful for sick people, and I use a great deal of it in the year."

"Oh, thank you, sir!"

"Gather plenty of it, Wavie; for it is as easy to dry and bleach a good quantity, as a mere handful; and perhaps you can sell what I don't want, at Miramore, with your cockles and mussels."

"Oh, yes; and thank you, sir!" said Wavie again, her cheeks bright with a warm flush of joy and her face a perfect picture of gladness. A very pretty picture, Dr. Doran thought it, though something in its delicate coloring awoke his professional fears.

"That child won't be long for earth," he said to himself, as he rode carefully down the rugged footpath. "She needs as much care and sheltering as one of the Duke's camellias, or I am greatly mistaken; and here she is knocking about, like any little mountain-born thing, with a nature like yonder whin bush. I wonder where she came from and whose child she really is. Those graceful limbs of hers tell of gentle blood; and her face is innocent, and thoughtful enough to have served as a study for one of Raphael's angels. This wild Glenderg is a strange home for one like her; I greatly fear it will prove in the end to be too rough and rude for the tender little thing. I wonder if there is any chance of tracing her people by advertisements in the English and American papers! But the child seems happy enough where she is; I doubt if the grandest relations in the world would suit her better than those good Creigans; I only wish she was a bit stronger!"

Wavie had run back to tell Margaret what the doctor had said about the carageen. "Now, mother, there is something I can do, at last!"

"At last, is it?" and the blind woman passed her hand lovingly over the little face upturned to her, as Wavie knelt at her side. The caressing movement so habitual to her, it seemed as though she sought by her sense of touch to know the form and expression of the childish features which she had never seen, and never could see. Wavie caught her hand in both her own; "Yes, mother, at last! I have been thinking so long what I could do to help you and father."

"I tell you once, ahaska, that you do help, and help well; don't go for to make me say it again; the father might hear, and it would worrit him, ye see."

Antony had heard. He called Wavie to him, and when

she came he drew down the golden head until its tresses rested against his rough cheek. "You are a blessing to us all, child, and in the future to come you will be blessed."

Chapter 11
ON THE SHORE

O wen! Owen! Can you come to the rocks with us?" called Wavie, from the road at the bottom of the valley, to Owen, who was busily spreading seaweed on one of his mother's fields—seaweed which was to serve as manure for next year's crop.

Owen stood still for a minute, resting on his pitchfork. Poor boy! He looked woefully tired; he would have rejoiced to throw down that heavy fork and join the little group, but he shook his head.

"I'm afeared I can't just now, Wavie," he answered; "there's a power here to spread yet. Ye see I'm trying to keep mother from feeling the lack of Antony's help in the fields; but faith! I never knew how much he did for us before."

"Can't you come, then?" said Madge, dolefully; "there's never any fun when you're not with us."

"Besides, Owen, I want you to show me where the carageen grows, that you got for Dr. Doran. I am going to gather some, and bleach it if you will show me how, and he has promised to buy it from me. But I don't know what it's like yet; the doctor told me you know."

"And that I do! None better, but it only grows on them low black rocks, at the very end of Ennis Point; the tide won't be out that far for this half hour, so, maybe, I will get through with my work in that spell of time, and I'll come and join ye if I can."

So Owen worked away manfully while Wavie, Madge, and Dennis clambered over the slippery rocks in search of the shellfish they had come out to obtain. They turned up the brown tufts of wrack round the edges of the pools to find the shy periwinkles, or picked them out from the bottom of the shallow limpid water—funny little horned fellows are these "winkles," carrying their black shells on their backs in true snail fashion. Indeed, sea snails they are, nothing more, nor less. The limpets are very different in their habits and appearance. The children sought them on the rocks which the waves had worn smooth and even, where their pointed shells looked like tiny Chinese sugar-loaf hats—only without any brim. Some favorite rocks were studded as thickly as nails are driven upon a church door, and here was a fine harvest for the old thin knives with which Margaret had provided them. The limpet clings with wonderful strength to its rocky home; sometimes in its hours of feeding, or breathing, the creature hangs loosely enough, and a sudden jerk will easily detach it; but once alarm it, and expelling all the air from its interior, the sharp edges of the shell close down like a vice, and then strong fingers, dashing waves, and fishes on foraging expeditions may try in vain to force it from its hold.

There was a rushing, tumbling, mountain stream which ran through the valley of Glenderg; and up the mouth of this "river"—as it was termed—the finest mussels were to be found. So there, among the stones, the children clambered, setting their knives to work in the narrow crevices this time, where the dark-blue shells were wedged. Strong fellows these mussels were; and sometimes they would have quite a fight with one tough old one, who had managed to grow in so narrow and awkward a corner, that even the thin blades of the children's weapons could hardly scoop him out.

When they were tired of shellfish hunting, they sat themselves down to wait for Owen, on a rock where they could watch the dark-colored water of the stream run down to meet the tide. They thought it great fun to watch the waves battling with the river—to see the frothy crests rise up in a mimic storm, as the separate forces clashed: nor was the conquest so very unequal; for the tide was low, and the sea was calm, so the river did not have such a fight for its own way as usual. But the ripple and the rush were quite enough to please the children who sat watching there; for they had no costly mechanical toys, no gorgeously dressed waxen dolls, to help to while away their hours of play; they were accustomed only to such playthings as they could find on the mountain, or on the shore; and, maybe, they were happier than those whose only effort seems to be to devise some new wish to be fulfilled, some new possession to covet.

Owen was not very long in joining them; and then they went off to the end of Ennis Point to get the precious carageen moss. There it grew, in the beautiful pools left by the tide, with a curious prismatic hue on its dark, short fronds, something of the hue on a wood pigeon's neck.

"But will this stuff ever get white, Owen?" asked Wavie dubiously, as she detached a handful from its native rock.

"Ay, will it. Not to the whiteness of snow, but white it gets, surely. They boil it down in milk, the doctor says, and it's wonderful strengthening for sick folks."

"Shall we get much money for it, Owen?"

"The doctor gave me a whole shilling, he did, for a pound weight of it; but a pound is a pretty decent bag full, I can tell you, Wavie. It's light as feathers when it's dry."

"Well, there is plenty to be had of it here—just look at all that lot under yonder big stone!"

And then Wavie told Owen of her plan of taking some of their sea-spoils to Neil and asking him to carry them for sale to the grand people at Miramore. She told him so eagerly and happily that she did not notice his grave face, until she came to the end of her speech; then his look struck her.

"Don't you think anyone would buy such things there, Owen? The doctor thought they would."

But Owen shook his head.

"They might buy them fast enough, if there was anyone to sell them," he answered her; "but I'm certain sure Neil won't go round with baskets of them things; no, not if the Queen of England was to ax him. An' even supposing he did, why he'd spend every penny he got for them in whiskey, before ever he left the quay."

"Oh, dear!" and Wavie sat down on a smooth stone and looked helplessly at her companion. "I have been counting so much on that way of getting some money," she said, sadly.

"I could go with the baskets myself, only there is so much to be done in the fields just now. There is the last of the kelp to be burned, too; I don't rightly see how I could spend the whole day going all that piece. Then there's mother; she could go, only she's so busy at your house now Antony's lying."

Owen's suggestions didn't seem very useful since he himself so clearly demonstrated their impracticability; but Wavie's sorrowful face obliged him to say something—even if he couldn't find anything of a very helpful kind to say.

"Owen!" exclaimed she, starting to her feet, "why shouldn't I go?"

"You!"

"Go where, Wavie?" asked Madge—who had been wading

in a pool after some prawns and had managed to thoroughly
wet herself from her elf-like locks to her little bare toes—"Go
where?"

"To Miramore, to sell our shellfish and caragreen," replied
Wavie stoutly. "Why shouldn't I? I'm sure Neil will take
me."

"But think on the strange place it is, and you are not fit
to go alone into the rough world, so you're not!" objected
Owen, speaking as though Glenderg were some favored
haven where alone Wavie could be safe. "I wouldn't allow
you to go, not on no account!"

Wavie looked up at him and laughed. "What will hurt
me?" said she. "Come home now, for it is nearly suppertime,
and if we stay much longer mother will be fancying we are
all drowned. See, Owen!" she continued, as she lifted her
little creel on her shoulders, "I'll carry this on my back,
and that basket Dennis has in my hand, and a bag for the
caragreen (when it is dry)—and I will go round to every house
in Miramore rather than not get all sold!"

"Oh, it's not doubting your will that I am," he answered,
as he helped the little ones in their scramble over the big
stones, "but I'm thinking ye don't rightly know how far
the way is, and how strange and thronged them fine streets
be. Then Neil, and his old daft father-in-law, are no very
pretty companions for a wee thing like ye. Better give it up,
Wavie."

"Give it up? Give up my plan of getting silver shillings to
buy white bread, and flesh meat, and biscuits for father now
he is so dreadfully weak and ill! Oh no, Owen; don't say
that! I shall not like the long journey with Neil, nor the fine
streets, nor the strange people; but if there is no one but me
to go, why I'm sure our Father in Heaven will just be kind
enough to look after me. Don't you think He will, Owen?"

And Owen glanced at the bright face at his side, where

faith, hope, and love shone forth unclouded by one doubt
or fear; and then he looked up to the sky where the sunset
glow was deepening into the quiet tender hue of night, and
where one bright planet already hung, a glittering token of its
Maker's wondrous power. "Yes, Wavie," he said, very slowly
and reverently, "I think He will."

Chapter 12
NEIL'S BOAT

Miramore was a town, large enough to lay legitimate claim to the title. In the West of Ireland the country is divided into small parcels of land, each dignified by the name of "town," and even the smallest collection of cabins is always so designated by its inhabitants, to the no small mystification and amusement of the chance traveller who may wander through these unfrequented regions. But Miramore was quite an important place. Somebody with taste enough to appreciate its glorious scenery, and energy enough to take advantage of it, had built a picturesque and roomy hotel there. The venture was successful, for fashion in some incomprehensible freak had stamped the place with her seal of approval, and soon gaily dressed groups of loungers idled away the sunny hours on the strand; and the shaggy country ponies carried eager explorers up the heights and over the more distant sands. Lodging houses and shops sprang up speedily, and short rows of new houses followed in their wake. New houses with imposing stucco fronts, and doors resplendent in shining paint and bronze knockers. Miramore,

the little squalid seaport, was changing as if by enchantment
into the popular watering place of the northwestern coast,
and already huge letters announced cheap excursions by rail
and coach to this "delightful seaside retreat."

Many miles of coast lay between Miramore and Glenderg.
"Iron bound coast," as it would be termed in sailors'
parlance—lofty headlands running out long distances, from
the Bloody Foreland on the north, to Forman Head with its
tremendous cliffs, forming one side of Mira Bay. There was
no communication between the two places, for the simple
people of Glenderg had few dealings with the world beyond
"the mountains," excepting the link formed by the carriers'
carts, which took away their butter and eggs and brought
back the miscellaneous articles which filled the shelves of "the
shops." But these carts always went to Londonderry, which
was in an entirely opposite direction, so that as yet Miramore
seemed to them like an unknown land. And Owen was as
much startled when Wavie proposed going there in Neil's
kelp boat, as if she had announced her intention of voyaging
to "foreign kingdoms" at once.

Very, very early one morning, three or four days after the
children's talk upon the shore, Wavie was seated in the stern
of the heavily laden boat, holding aloft her little kerchief as a
farewell signal to Nelly and her son, who stood watching her
from the beach. She felt very hopeful and blithesome; and
looked down with innocent pride on her well-filled baskets,
and then back across the widening water to her friends—
shouting some loving message for Margaret as she did so. Her
foster father was much better; quite able to talk to them now,
and he had entered into all Wavie's plans and arrangements,
with such ready sympathy, and grateful appreciation of the
child's work of love, that her spirits had risen to their highest
point in glad anticipation. Margaret, too, had fondly blessed
her and called her the "blind woman's sunbeam"; and even

Owen, unwillingly as he saw her depart, forbore to say one
word which might cloud the smile upon her sweet bright face.

But when once fairly afloat upon the journey, out of
sight of the well-known rocks and sands of her home, the
little maiden felt lonely and anxious. Her companions were
not very pleasant-looking, even to her eyes, accustomed as
they were to rough visages and uncouth attire. Neil was a
decidedly ill-looking fellow; his small eyes glanced restlessly
from beneath his shaggy brows, the scar of some old wound
disfigured one cheek, and a coarse beard of at least a week's
growth did not add to his attractiveness. Yet he, untutored
and rough as he was, spoke gently to the child and had built
a little nest for her among his blocks of kelp, quite forgetful
that he had told Nelly Brennan when she asked for a passage
for Wavie and her baskets that "he wanted no useless lumber
clustering up his boat—that the gisseh had much better stay
where she was, than push herself where nobody had axed
her to come." His words had been quite as rough when
Nelly's expostulations had wrung from him his ungracious
permission; but now the presence of the fair tiny creature
seemed to melt his hard mood, like sunlight upon an iceberg.
His old father-in-law never once spoke to her, or seemed to
be aware of her presence. He was half-witted, people said; but
there was a look of cunning on his face which seemed to belie
the assertion. He sat in the bows of the boat sturdily pulling
his oar, looking neither to the right hand, nor the left, his
broken hat slouched over his eyes as if the bright beams of
the rising sun annoyed him.

Wavie's newly awakened fears came rushing over her
poor little heart, until she most sincerely wished herself
back at Glenderg. It was such a long way to Miramore, and
it would be so late when they returned. Owen was right, she
thought: Neil's boat was hardly a fitting place for her. She
turned her head and looked longingly back to Ennis Point,

and as she did so the beauty of the sunrise radiance caught
her attention. How beautiful it was! Down over the distant
hills it poured, till their edges seemed molten gold, against
the golden sky—down upon the moorlands, till the heather
caught the crimson fire and glowed crimson in reply—then
on over the water, touching and tinting each wave, even each
ripple, until they seemed to form a golden chain of flashing,
quivering glory.

Her lips parted with excitement as she gazed upon this
flood of brightness, poured, as it were, from the very hand of
God upon the awakening world. She remembered how in the
songs of the Psalmist the words were written: "The heavens
declare the glory of God, and the firmament showeth His
handiwork." She looked at the mountains, the "everlasting
hills," whose foundations seemed verily as if built upon the
seas and established upon the floods—and then her eye swept
the noble line of coast, with its giant cliffs and huge rocks
standing like sentinels out of the water, until her glance
rested on the western horizon, where the ocean spread on, on
to the very shores of that other hemisphere from whence she
had come. There was no living thing visible upon the shore;
there was no single sail upon the surface of the sea: nothing
in all that wide expanse to break the terrible solitude, except
the long-necked cormorants, commencing their day's fishing,
and the screaming gulls and kittiwakes, wheeling and floating
on the shallow water, where the sand banks stretched out
from beyond Carickarn. In the midst of the grandest scenes
of nature, Wavie was alone, save for those silent men at the
oars; but the sense of loneliness and fear was gone from the
child's heart, gone just as the white mist hanging over the
Bloody Foreland had broken and melted away in the light of
the beaming sun.

She no longer wished that she had not left Glenderg; she
saw the "works of the Lord and His wonders in the deep,"

and her doubt and the dread had passed away, while she heard—as in an echo—Antony's voice repeating one of his favourite verses: "This God is our God for ever and ever; He will be our guide even unto death."

Once out from the shelter of Ennis Point, the men shipped their oars and spread their tattered coffee-colored sail to the gentle breeze. Neil came stepping over the kelp blocks to his seat at the stern; but he gruffly told Wavie not to disturb herself, for he had plenty of room; and grasping the rudder with his horny hands, he forthwith relapsed into his former silence. Wavie soon forgot his very existence. She leant over the boat's side and trailed her rosy fingers through the foam. She watched the long graceful fronds of the floating seaweed moving with the moving water; and then she began to hum to herself, very softly and inarticulately at first, until half unconsciously she began to sing the children's hymn she had learnt when a mere baby in her Canadian home:

"Here we suffer grief and pain;
Here we meet to part again;
In heaven we part no more.
O! That will be joyful,
Joyful, joyful, joyful,
O! That will be joyful
When we meet to part no more!

"All who love the Lord below
When they die to heaven will go,
And sing with saints above.
O! That will be joyful
When we meet to part no more!

"O! How happy we shall be,
For our Saviour we shall see

Exalted on His throne.
O! That will be joyful
When we meet to part no more!

"There we all shall sing with joy,
And eternity employ
In praising Christ the Lord."

Sweetly and softly over the sea rang the refrain, and the
rough men gazed at her with astonishment as she sang:

"O! That will be joyful,
Joyful, joyful, joyful,
O! That will be joyful
When we meet to part no more!"

"What kind of words are them?" demanded Neil,
suddenly—so suddenly that Wavie started at his voice.

"It's a hymn," she answered him, timidly.

"But ye spoke of the saints—glory be to the same!—and I
thought ye Protestants didn't hold with them at all?"

Wavie was hardly prepared for controversy. "It says in
God's book that they are in heaven praising God," she
replied, "and my hymn says we shall join them there when we
die. Good people are saints, you know."

"Well, I never heard much about them anyways; but your
song is a pretty song; and it can't rightly be a bad song when
it speaks of the saints. Ye might sing it again; it'll do ye no
harm, nor we neither."

So Wavie sang it again and then one after another of her
hymns, but Neil heard them without further remark.

Easily and swiftly glided the kelp boat over the sunny
sea with its strangely assorted freight: the hardened vicious
men, whose intellects were only exerted for the sake of drink

and greed, who lived their lives as the animals live, with no
thought for aught beyond and the fair, guileless child, who
had already learned such lessons of love, love to those humble
friends who owned no ties of kindred blood, but who were
yet so near, and dear—and love to the great God, Whose
blessed Son had taught the fishermen of Galilee to call Him
"Our Father."

Chapter 13
First Earnings

The glorious sun, which had shone so warmly all that October day, had long ago sank down behind the sea, and soft grey clouds were creeping up from the west and hiding the faint starlight. Wavie, with Madge and Owen, was coming up the hill; her step was eager, and her voice had the happy cadence so peculiarly her own. Since sunset Owen and the children had been waiting on the shore; but Neil's boat was long in coming, so long indeed that Nelly had carried off the sleepy Dennis to his little straw bed and even attempted to coax Madge to accompany her also. But the little girl was not to be persuaded; she would "stay until Wavie came, for she had promised her to do so."

Owen felt very anxious as he stood there, leaning against a large block of stone which rested on the pier. What could detain Neil so long? Had he taken too much whiskey again? And had evil befallen the boat which held the fairy "sunbeam" so dear to Glenderg? The waves came whispering up against the shore with a mournful monotony, and the sea birds on the cliffs now and then sent their wild ghastly cries

echoing over the water. With the poetry of temperament so
strongly developed in the national character, these sounds,
slight as they were, affected Owen powerfully. His face looked
so pale and stern in the cold evening light that Madge noticed
its expression.

"When do you think they'll be coming?" she asked, more
for the sake of breaking the painful silence than of hearing
his reply.

He did not answer her, but rose to his feet, listening
intently, and peering out to sea.

"There's the boat! At last she is coming!" and Madge
clapped her hands and joyfully echoed "she's coming!"

"Oh, Wavie, I've been fearsome for ye, darlint," said
Owen, as she sprang on the steps of the quay.

"Why?" she returned, "didn't I say that our Father in
Heaven would take good care of me? You shouldn't have
troubled about me, Owen. Oh, take the baskets, and let us
run home; I've got such a lot of pennies! You must count
them for me."

She waited on the pier to thank Neil for his "kindness";
but he made no acknowledgment of her gratitude, beyond an
inarticulate growl. He was busy with the cordage of the boat
and perhaps had scarcely heard her. Neil's gruffness had no
effect upon her now; she was too happy in being home again,
too elated at her success, too eager to reach her foster parents,
for her spirits to be easily damped. She looked in at Nelly's
door as they passed and called out—

"I've got such a great deal of money, Nelly dear; aren't you
glad? I've sold all my cargo, as father called it, goodnight!"
And then the child ran on by Owen's side, skipping and
bounding up the path to her home.

"Mother, mother! Just feel the weight of it. It's all for you!"
And thrusting into Margaret's hands her little handkerchief—
in which her coppers, her first precious earnings, were

knotted up—she crossed the floor to Antony's bedside,
to receive his welcoming words and to tell the tale of her
adventures.

She had met with much kindness in Miramore and a ready
sale for her shellfish among the "quality" visiting there. One
old lady had asked her questions concerning her home and
had sent a bright shilling to her sick father.

"She spoke so gently to me, father," said Wavie, "and she
looked so beautiful in her shining black dress and white hair.
She was sitting on a seat upon the shore, with a little girl by
her side—a little girl not any bigger than me."

"And when ye saw the grand folks did ye wish that ye had
never been wrecked on the coast of Glenderg?" asked Antony,
looking a little sadly on the sweet face of his foster daughter.
"Did ye remember the time when ye too wore shining gowns
and was waited on daintily and reared with care? Did ye—"

"Yes, father," she interrupted him quickly, "I did
remember the time; but I didn't wish that I had never seen
Glenderg; for before I came here no one really loved me,
except poor Catherine. You see I was not uncle Frank's
own little girl, and of course he and Auntie liked their own
children best; but here I am so happy, for I know you love
me, don't you father? And as for dresses—this one is much
better to wear than a silk one, for I could not gather mussels
and cockles in that for fear of splashing it."

"There'd be no need to gather such things if ye had your
rights, Wavie."

"Father, you are very silly tonight! I tell you I am rich, so
rich! Don't you see all that money Owen is counting out? It is
better to get that than to wear silk dresses, isn't it?"

"Child, you've catched cold," said the blind woman, whose
quick ear had remarked the short dry cough which broke so
often on Wavie's talk.

"Only a little, mother; it will be gone in the morning."

"Come, get ye to bed now; ye must be fairly tired out. I'll
bring ye a cup of hot milk and your roasted 'praties when
you're lying down; if ye stay here, ye'll chatter till daylight."

So Wavie went into "the room," as it was always termed;
and before she threw herself on her rude crib, she knelt to
offer her earnest thanks to the Father in Heaven, who had
had watchful care over her through all that eventful day.
Margaret was delayed a few minutes in attending to Antony's
wants; when she came with the potatoes and milk, she knew
by Wavie's peaceful measured breathing that, worn out by
the unusual excitement she had undergone, she had already
fallen asleep. Margaret stood by her bedside and passed her
hand lovingly over little Madge's shock of straight brown
hair. She did not dare to touch Wavie's fair tresses for fear of
awakening her, but very deep and fervent was the blessing she
uttered as she bent over the two children. Again she noticed
the cough which shook Wavie's frame; and she anxiously laid
her shawl above the scanty bedclothes—that same red shawl
which had wrapt her round the day when Antony bore her
first to his cabin out of the power of the sea and the storm.

Three years had gone by since the wreck of the Queen of
the Wave; and they had been eventful years to the Creigans.
Margaret had passed them in her darkness and comparative
helplessness. She had never looked on the sunlight, never
seen her children as they grew up by her side, never knew
what Wavie's face could be, when bright with happiness or
tender and grave with the thoughtfulness which so often
shadowed it. And yet Margaret had not been miserable nor
gloomy in her blindness. Bitter trial as it was, she knew now
that it had been exactly the chastening that her spirit needed.
She could not murmur for the loss of her bodily sight, when
God had revealed to her something of the breadth, and
length, and depth, and height of the love of Christ, which
passeth knowledge. And this new trial, Antony's terrible

accident, coming as it did in their poverty and distress, would it not have some good hidden behind the dark cloud? Yes, Margaret could believe and trust now; and could turn from dwelling on her sorrows to counting up God's mercies. And chiefest amongst these—her many blessings—she reckoned the stranger-child, who for these three years past had been to her as a daughter, Agatha Buchanan, her own Wavie.

Chapter 14
ADA SOMERSET

Each time Neil's boat went on the long voyage to Miramore, Wavie and her baskets were to be seen in their place at the stern. The boatmen were taciturn and glum as ever, but yet the child always found a sheltered nook among the kelp blocks arranged for her; and when the sea was rough, and the spray rose high, an old tarpaulin, or the end of the sail, was always drawn across so as to shield her from being saturated by the sharply-flung drops. Seated there, bound on her journey of love, she would sing over and over again her store of hymns and songs—singing as the larks sing because her heart was glad, and the music of praise was its natural form of expression.

She did not know that Neil listened to her as he had never listened to anything of good before; she did not know that her simple lays were the only glimpse of heaven, and truth, and Jesus which had ever shone on that dark heart. It was true that Neil's broad shoulders and heavy brows might often be seen in the chapel in "the town," but he went there because he shared the superstition of his countrymen

and believed that if he did not keep on the "right side of
the priest" it would be worse for him in the next world.
The only religion he had ever heard of was a very different
thing to the spirit breathed forth by Wavie's hymns. There
was much in them, simple as they were, that was beyond
his comprehension; there was much that astonished and
bewildered him; but there was also much that penetrated
beneath the crust of depravity and ignorance to the soil
beneath—seed dropped at random by a tiny hand, but which
might hereafter take root in the hard nature, and spring
up, and bear fruit a hundredfold. It has often been so. It
shall often be so! For the truth still stands as it was written
two thousand years ago: "Out of the mouths of babes and
sucklings Thou has perfected praise."

But the autumn was passing away, those bright October
days which have won for the month the name of the
"Donegal summer." Soon Neil would go no more to
Miramore; soon the gay visitors would be departing; and
soon, too, the cockles and winkles and such like "small
game" would be out of season and useless. The subject cost
Wavie much anxious thought; at present she could see no
other plan for gaining money; she must make the best of
her shellfish and her carageen, while she could gather and
sell them, and trust that during the coming wintertime, Dr.
Doran or Owen, or her own little brains, might hit on some
other plan of earning the pennies which were so welcome in
her foster parents' cottage.

Dear little Wavie! She did not then know that before the
winter snows came to whiten the brown moorlands, she
should have passed to that "better country" where there shall
be no more toil, nor sorrow, nor sighing—or that before the
last leaves fell from the Fairy-tree by Lough Illion, the dear
friends she loved so well would need her aid no longer.

One morning, the first gloomy day that had come for

many weeks, Wavie ascended the steps of the pretentious houses in Alexandra Terrace, a new row of stuccoed buildings, standing perilously near to the edge of the cliff. This was the last call she had to make; her baskets were nearly empty, and the little handkerchief in which she tied up her money had grown bulky and heavy with the coppers it contained.

"We aren't wanting any of that sort of rubbish," said a dapper manservant, who answered her timid pull at the bell; "we never buy things at the door."

"But I have often brought my shellfish here—"

"More shame for you, then!" interrupted the man, as he proceeded to shut the door in her face.

"Oh, please!" pleaded Wavie, the tears coming to her eyes at his roughness, "please, Mrs. Somerset told me to call the next time I came to Miramore."

"Ho, indeed! Then I suppose you'd better go through to the kitchen. Though why missus wants that nasty trash, that she never eats, is more than I can make out."

This latter remark was made in an undertone, as the man marched to the back premises, leaving Wavie—laden as she was with her baskets—to battle as best she might with the swinging door.

"Here is the money for your shellfish," said a shy voice, when the cook had measured out a certain quantity. "Grandmamma has a headache, so she sent me to ask you how your father is today." And the servant stood aside as a little girl came up to the kitchen table—the same little girl whom Wavie had seen on the shore with the lady in the "shining dress."

"And grandmamma told me to ask you what your name is," was the next remark, when Wavie had replied to her question concerning Antony.

"My name is Agatha, but everybody calls me 'Wavie.'"

"What a funny name! Why do they call you so?" inquired the little lady, growing more at her ease as she came under the influence of that sweet face, with its gentle eyes.

"Because my real name, 'Agatha,' seemed hard for them to say; and as I was wrecked in a ship called the Queen of the Wave, somehow Dennis first, and then everybody else, began to call me 'Wavie.'"

"And you were really wrecked! Do tell me all about it."

Wavie hesitated. Her instinctive good feeling told her this was hardly the time or place to enter into a long history relating so exclusively to herself. Besides, she caught the eyes of the disagreeable manservant fixed on her with a sneering, doubting expression, which made the hot blood come into her cheeks. Even to her childish inexperience, it was plain that he considered her either an imposter or something nearly approaching thereto.

"Oh, do tell me how you were wrecked!" said Ada Somerset, again. "Sit down here on this chair, and begin. I shall like to hear it all, for I've never seen the sea before, and I want to know about it. I've often read of wrecks, but I've never seen anybody who has been wrecked. Do tell me everything!"

Thus pressed, Wavie told the story in the fewest possible words. Of the storm of that terrible night she could say nothing, for she recollected little of it; but she related how she had been found almost dead from cold and exposure on the shore; and then she went on to speak of the kind, brave Antony and his blind wife, with all the affection of her grateful heart. She told how the terrible accident had befallen her foster father, how the potatoes were all bad, and how sorely she had wished to earn money. And then, her tone changing, and her eyes brightening, she told the little English lady how she had succeeded: how Madge and Dennis had helped her in getting the shellfish; how Owen had shown her how to gather and dry the carageen moss; and how she had got for them "so many, many pennies" to carry home to Glenderg.

Ada Somerset listened with keenest interest. Her life had been spent hitherto in a quiet old-fashioned city in the West of England, or in an Italian town almost as quiet, where Mrs. Somerset had been obliged to go on account of ill-health. Her parents were in India; she had lived, ever since she could recollect, with her grandmother, who had striven to foster every kind and sympathetic feeling of her nature and had taught her, young as she was, that life was something more than mere selfish enjoyment—that the highest and purest happiness is to be found in striving to create happiness for others. "This romance in real life," which she had accidentally drawn out, affected her powerfully. The story, told so simply, and unhesitatingly, was quite as interesting as any contained in the gaily bound volumes which filled her own little bookshelves at home—nay, far more so, for it was really true, and there stood the heroine actually before her! Then a better feeling than that of excited childish curiosity was aroused within her. She had listened to a tale of the real sorrow and privation which she dimly knew existed in the world—far as it hitherto had been from her own bright path—and as she listened she longed to render some help towards lightening the burden pressing so heavily on Wavie's tiny shoulders.

Her thoughts flew to her netted green silk purse which reposed in her drawer upstairs. It contained three sovereigns, the gift of her godfather on her last birthday, and as yet she had not been tempted to spend them. How much they could do for Wavie, and the Creigans! But she shrank from offering the money before the servants, for bare-footed and scantily-clothed as Wavie was, her manner was as gentle and graceful as Ada's own. Besides she knew that Jones, the butler, would regard the story she had just heard as a mere appeal for help;

and this Ada knew was very far from the truth.

While she stood pondering, Wavie had quietly taken up her baskets.

"Good bye, Miss," she said, "please tell the lady that I am sorry her head is aching and that I'm much obliged to her for taking my winkles."

"You will come again?" said Ada. "We are not going home for a long time yet, though grandmamma talks of leaving Miramore on a trip round the coast before we go back to England; but surely we shall see you again."

"I don't quite know if I shall be coming again, Miss. Neil, who brings me over in his boat, has sold all his kelp, except a very little, that is hardly worth the carrying; but if he comes, I'll come too; and I'll bring you the finest periwinkles I can find on all the shore."

Ada followed Wavie to the street door. It had been a dreary, lowering morning; and now the wind had risen, and cold rain was splashing down pitilessly. It seemed dreadful to the child of wealth and luxury that one as young and frail as herself should have to brave the cold and wet, unprotected by any of the wraps which were always at her own command. The feeling of sympathy and love came again over her heart, and in a moment of unreasoning impulse, she turned from the open door, dashed upstairs, and came flying down again, her treasured green silk purse in her hand. The housemaid was closing the door, but Ada breathlessly pushed it open, and in her haste would have sprung out into the rain after Wavie, but for the servant's restraining hand.

"I'll soon call her back, Miss; don't you venture into that teem of rain," said the maid; and raising her voice, she made it reach Wavie's ears, even through the noise of the wind.

"I wanted to give you this," said Ada, hurriedly, thrusting her treasure into Wavie's hand as she spoke. "You need not look at it now, and don't say 'Thank you,' for really I have no need for it, and I shall be so glad if it helps you a little. Goodbye!" And the English girl went back to the sitting room, her heart overflowing with its newly-found interest and with the keen sense of the delight there is in the blessed work of "well-doing."

God has knitted human souls very closely by His Divine links of love and sympathy. Worldly "wisdom," selfishness, and sin sunder them far: snapping the links ruthlessly, until the "new commandment" given by our Lord is as a dead letter, a forgotten thing; and the words "that ye love one another" sound alien and strange. Ada was too young yet to have any misgivings as to what she had done. She had not yet learnt to be distrustful and suspicious. She did not need her three bright sovereigns, and that Wavie did appeared to her quite sufficient reason for giving them to her. To be able to afford her help in her work for the suffering Antony, and the blind Margaret, seemed to Ada ample return for the gift.

She longed to be able to talk it all over with somebody who could suggest any plans for the benefit of the family at Glenderg, but she had to learn a lesson of patience that afternoon. Worn out by hours of pain, her grandmamma lay sleeping on the sofa; and Elizabeth, her confidential maid—who was often the little girl's counsellor and helper— had gone out on some errand for her mistress. So Ada sat on the window seat gazing out into the rain and curbed her impatience as best she might. Whilst Wavie hastened on her way to the boat, regardless of the weather, tripping over the sharp stones with her little bare feet; and in spite of wind and rain, and in spite of the rough path, she felt happy and joyous, with the little lady's gift in her hand and the memory of the gift of sweet sympathy in her heart.

Chapter 15
PAST DAYS

It was not until after tea that Mrs. Somerset was able to leave her couch and sit by the peat fire, which had been lighted more for the sake of its cheeriness than for its warmth; and then Ada brought a cushion to her feet, and resting her arms on the old lady's knee, launched at once into the history of the Foundling of Glenderg.

"That little girl, you know, granny, who brings the shellfish for sale, and whom you often speak to—"

"What did you say her name is?" almost screamed Mrs. Somerset, grasping her startled grandchild by the shoulder.

"'Agatha,' I think she said; but what is the matter, dear granny?"

"And what was the name of the ship she was wrecked in?" demanded the lady, still in the same excited tone, and not noticing Ada's question in the least. "What did she say the ship's name was?"

"The Queen of the Wave, and they called her 'Wavie' because of it. But do tell me what you know about it all, won't you, granny dear?"

Mrs. Somerset had sunk back again in her chair and covered her face with her hands, and Ada gazed at her in silence.

"I came to find her grave, if I could," she said at last, speaking to herself in a low, broken voice; "can it indeed be that she lives still? How strange if it should indeed be so! And yet there seems but little reason to doubt. How long is it since the shipwreck, Ada?"

"I don't know, grandmamma; but it must be a long, long time, as so much has happened since."

Mrs. Somerset smiled, even at that moment of intense emotion, at the idea of a "long, long time" having passed, either in Ada's short life, or in Wavie's. "Did she say where she lived?" was her next question.

"Yes, but I quite forgot now. It was 'Glen' something or other, I think."

There was a long pause. The firelight shone on Mrs. Somerset's troubled face, where the shadows of many sorrows had left lines on the broad forehead and dimmed the kindly eyes, once so clear and brilliant. Large tears hung on the eyelids now; and Ada noticing them, held her peace. What could have moved her grandmother so powerfully, she wondered. She longed to utter the questions which came thronging to her lips, but she restrained the impulse, although the effort cost the eager child every atom of her self-control. Her reward came at last, for Mrs. Somerset roused herself, and laying her hand on Ada's hair, said softly:

"Do you remember the picture hanging above my writing table in my own room, at home, Ada? A young girl, dressed in white, with roses in her arms and at her feet."

"You mean aunt Eleanor's picture, granny! Yes, of course, I remember it; but what can that have to do with Wavie?"

"Listen to me, Ada, and I will try and tell you—though it all seems so strange and impossible that I can hardly realize it even now." Again the old lady paused and gazed into the fire, silently; and when the minutes went by, one after another, and still she did not speak, Ada ventured to say, as a gentle reminder:

"Yes, grandmamma, dear?"

"Your aunt Eleanor was my only daughter, and she was very, very dear to me. She was between nineteen and twenty when your father brought one of his brother officers from India to spend part of his furlough with us. I never liked him from the first. He was handsome and winning, it is true, but I saw he was selfish and proud, and I grieved to see the hold he had obtained over Harry. Therefore, I was glad to hear that your father had exchanged into another regiment and that their firm friendship would thus be interrupted. But the time soon came when I wished passionately that Captain Buchanan had never returned from India—that he had gone anywhere, so that it was far from our home in Aylchester. He came to see us often after that first long visit, and he told me at last what I had dreaded for months: he and Eleanor loved one another, and he asked me to give her to him. It was true that she loved him, and I could deny her nothing; so they were married. They seemed very happy, and in their happiness I tried to forget my gloomy forebodings; but I could not succeed. The garrison town was within an easy distance of Aylchester, and I often saw my darling; and I thought that I perceived she was beginning to discover that her husband was not the high-souled hero she had fancied him to be, but that he was not walking with her in spirit along the narrow way that our Saviour's steps have sanctified.

"Within a year of their marriage, Captain Buchanan's regiment was ordered to Canada; and I had to part from my only daughter—to part from her forever on earth. Her health was not strong, and the voyage tried her severely. Captain Buchanan had a brother settled in Canada, and to his house he took her. They did everything which was in their power, no doubt; but it was wintertime, and the cruel cold was too much for her delicate frame. Not many weeks afterwards, I received a letter to tell me it was all over—that she had given her sweet life back into God's hands—that I might never look upon her face again, until—which God grant!—I meet her in our Father's kingdom above.

"She left a baby behind her: a little girl; but Captain Buchanan could not bear the sight of it. He desired that it should not even be called after her name; so she was christened 'Agatha' after his own mother. You start, Ada! Yes, I believe our poor little shellfish girl is really your cousin Agatha Buchanan."

"Oh, grandmamma!"

"The child was left in her uncle's charge," continued Mrs. Somerset, "and her father returned to his regimental duties. I have never seen him since, but they tell me he is little altered. The same charm of manner, the same quiet self-assertion distinguished him still. Eleanor was the one thing, besides himself, that he had ever dearly loved; and I do not believe that he has forgotten her. He writes to me sometimes; cold, short letters they are, but I can tell from their very forcedness and brevity that he loves her no whit less deeply than the day he took her from my side.

"My home in Aylchester was very dreary until you, dear child, came from India, to be cared for and loved; and then the thought occurred to me that if I had the little Agatha, my Eleanor's child, with me also, that it would be well for you, for her, and for myself. I wrote to Major Buchanan, as he was then (he is a Colonel now), but before his answer came I was taken seriously ill, as you may remember, Ada; and we were obliged to go to Italy for the winter. When we were settled there, I wrote again about Agatha's joining me. Her father gave a ready consent to my request, and the child and her nurse set out for England under the care of a Captain Royston; and his ship was the Queen of the Wave.

"I sent Elizabeth to meet her at Liverpool, and she and the child were to join us at Mentone, travelling under the escort of some friends of mine, who were on their way to Rome. I waited anxiously for news of the ship's arrival, but instead of what I was waiting and hoping for, Elizabeth arrived alone, bringing me a copy of the 'Times' containing an account of the total wreck of the Queen of the Wave, with the terrible words 'all on board lost.' There seemed nothing remaining for me to do. I see now that I should have come here to Donegal at once, or, if my health would have rendered that impossible, at any rate urged Major Buchanan to do so, that due inquiries should be made concerning the fate of the child. But such a thought never occurred to me then. I accepted the truth of that dreadful sentence with but one questioning doubt; and now after nearly three years I have come here, not to seek trace of her as living, but to know if the sea had held her body, or, if she had been laid in a nameless grave—to place a monument to mark the resting place of my Eleanor's daughter."

"Was that why you came to this strange, wild place, granny? You never told me anything of this," said Ada half-reproachfully.

"You were too young, dear, to understand this when it happened, and besides the story was full of such pain to me that I shrank from relating it to you needlessly. Yes, that was the reason I decided to come here this year. I have been weak and ill ever since that severe illness three years ago and have never felt equal to undertake the journey before now, though, as you know, I have almost day by day purposed to do so. Even since our arrival at Miramore, I have let days and weeks slip by and have never yet accomplished my purpose, though they tell me we are within thirty miles of the spot where the

wreck took place. Thirty miles by road, hardly more than
ten by sea. Oh, to think that I have lingered on here idly and
only learnt by chance the blessed news I might have heard
long ago. I shall never cease to blame myself! It seems difficult
now to wait quietly until the morning comes, and I can go
to her. If it had not been for my neglect and delay, she would
be with us here safe and warm now, instead of only sheltered
from this raging storm by some rude cottage. I pray God she
may have even reached that shelter in safety! Oh, Ada, I shall
never forgive myself."

"Dear grandmamma!" and Ada pressed her lips fondly
on the hand she held. Her fears for Wavie were also keenly
roused, and she shuddered as the loud blast shook the
casement of the window and came roaring from over the
roaring sea. There was silence between them for a time, and
then Ada asked about Colonel Buchanan.

"He is in England now," replied Mrs. Somerset; "he
returned from abroad a month or two ago. He wrote me a
strange letter in reply to mine about the wreck. 'If I was a
religious man,' he wrote, 'I should thank God heartily that
He withheld me from loving my child as a father ought to
have done. My heart could hardly have endured the blow
this would then have been to me, but as it now is, my great
sorrow is still my one sorrow. For the child herself I know
that this is best; she is safe now, beyond all danger, beyond all
temptations; and the motherless girl of a regimental officer
has always a difficult lot.' I echoed his words, 'it is best for the
child,' but I grieved sorely, nevertheless, that I had never held
her in my arms, never gazed upon her face.

"I know now what it was that drew me so strangely to that
little bare-footed girl. I know now why her great soft eyes
haunted me—why her face seemed familiar, as is the memory
of a dream."

"Dearest granny, you must not cry now; you are rich, for

you have two grandchildren instead of one now; and Wavie
is so pretty and sweet, I feel as if I loved her already. We shall
take her home with us, shan't we granny? How charming that
will be!"

"Ada," said the lady, "it is past your bedtime, dear; leave
me now; I must be alone."

Chapter 16
Firelight

For hours after the little girl had left her goodnight kiss on her grandmother's cheek, the old lady sat there by the dying fire, her mind filled with the recollections that evening's discovery had so unexpectedly stirred. Long illness had unstrung a nature once remarkable for its self-possession; and now, with no human eye to witness her weakness, Mrs. Somerset let the blinding tears have unrestrained course at last; and, resting her forehead on the cushioned back of her chair, she sobbed as she had not sobbed since the day when Eleanor had left her to go on board the troopship by her husband's side.

Mrs. Somerset had sometimes been spoken of as a "strong-minded woman," and many of her friends in Aylchester would have been greatly astonished could they have seen her now.

Early left a widow, with ample means and a recognized position, she had been looked up to as quite a leader in the society of the West country town where she resided. Her home was old and roomy, containing massive oaken furniture

of a date long gone by and dingy portraits of bewigged
gentlemen and powdered ladies gazing down from its walls.
Her garden was long and narrow, mathematically divided
by well-rolled gravel walks and full of standard rose bushes
and huge grey masses of fragrant lavender. Nothing new or
gaudy was to be found in her domain: fashionable petunias
and calceolarias would have appeared as much out of place
amongst the clipped yews and stately hollyhocks of her garden
as chrome lithographs and painted photographs would have
looked upon the dark panels of her sitting rooms.

Her sons had done her credit hitherto, and she was proud
of them, as well she might be. Richard, her firstborn, held a
family living: a model parish, with a model parsonage, buried
amongst the bowery lanes of Gloucestershire. Harry, Ada's
father, was an officer in India; he had married as befitted
a Somerset, and his mother, in her daydreams, built up a
golden future for him. Aleck—to whom an uncle had left an
independent income—was at the present time travelling in
Africa, seeing a little of the world, as he phrased it, before
he settled down to quiet English life. They were fine men, all
three of them, with their mother's handsome features and
genial manners—men who were fully aware of their position
in the world and who were prepared to act so as to adorn it.

Very different from her brothers was the youngest child,
"sweet Eleanor," as they fondly termed her. All the mother's
softer and gentler feelings were centered in the young girl
whose presence had brightened the stately old house like May
sunshine—whose laughter had rung out clear as a thrush's
song in the formal gardens, the bright-haired girl who had
always been the boys' pet and plaything—the fairest, and the
blithest thing in all the world to the widow.

Sitting now alone in the parlor of the lodging house at
Miramore, she seemed to lose the consciousness of the actual
present in the memories of the past. She heard, in fancy,

her Eleanor's step coming flying down the long corridor at
Aylchester; she seemed to feel the touch of her clinging hand
and the shower of her kisses. The hoarse voice of the storm
and the sobbing of the sea, beating on the Donegal coast,
changed, for her, to the whisper and rustle of the elm trees
in Aylchester Close and the music of the old cathedral bells
upon a Sabbath morning. No one event—no one special
hour—came to her mind as she sat there, but the old home
life seemed to be hers again, the life when "Home" was
worthy the name, not merely the abiding place, with the
aching sense of loss, which it had since become. She raised
her head, and smiles came to her lips, and a soft, happy
expression to her face, as she gave the rein to her fancy.

But "fancy" is poor comfort at best. The first bitterness
of her agony woke again in the bereaved mother's heart. She
had not that living rejoicing faith which can "rob the grave of
victory, and take the sting from death" for others than those
who themselves must enter the grave and feel the sting. Her
faith was enough to bid her hope, but not enough to whisper
"Peace." Her religion had been one of sentiment, and self-
satisfaction, and was neither real enough nor loving enough
to comfort her now. It is only those who live very close to the
feet of our Lord who can joyfully believe, as Wavie believed,
in the love of our Father in Heaven. We are so prone to forget
that the Master of the Kingdom has said, that, unless we
become as "little children we shall in no wise enter therein,"
as children in trustfulness and in unquestioning rest on
that Almighty Love. The richly bound Bible, which lay on
the center table at the lady's side, though it was read daily
with Ada and aloud to the assembled household morning
and night at Aylchester, was as an unknown book to her,
compared with what the smoke-stained one in its tattered
calf-skin cover was to Antony and Margaret in their cabin at
Glenderg.

Mrs. Somerset intended to do great things for the grandchild she had received again, as it were from the grave. She would take her from squalor and poverty and place her amidst all that wealth and taste could procure. Her threadbare garments should be replaced by daintiest linen and warmest wrappings. Instead of taking those long journeys to Miramore in an open boat, and with rude companions, she should have carriages and horses at her command and servants to obey her behests and anticipate her slightest wants—no more an uncared for peasant child, but filling her rightful place in her grandmother's home and heart, as the only child of the beloved Eleanor. Mrs. Somerset would have been startled could she have looked into the future and read the truth—could she have known that Wavie would never claim one of all these things and that she herself would learn from those childish lips the reality of the truths she thought she knew so well already; through Wavie she should become an inheritor of far higher and nobler things than human eye has seen, or human ear has heard.

The clock upon the mantle shelf pointed to near midnight. There was a knock at the door, and her maid Elizabeth entered.

"I beg your pardon, madam; but I thought you might have dropped asleep, as it was so late, and you had not rung."

The servant's presence aroused her from the thoughts, half sad ones, half happy ones, which she had been indulging in so long.

"Elizabeth," she said, "have you heard?"

"Yes, ma'am; Miss Ada told me. It is fairly wonderful and almost passes belief, as one may say. To think that that poor little thing should be Miss Eleanor's child!"

"That poor little thing," repeated Mrs. Somerset wearily.

"Yes, 'poor' indeed! Shoeless, and cold, and hungry! It drives me wild to think of it. We shall leave tomorrow, early, remember, early, Elizabeth, and fetch her here immediately. I shall not rest until I hold her in my arms. My Eleanor's child!"

Chapter 17
WAVIE'S LAST VOYAGE

Wife, I'm gettin' mighty uneasy concerning the child," said Antony, as a louder gust than any previous one came echoing down the sides of the mountain gorge. "I wish from my heart," he continued, "that she hadn't gone. I can't think where my eyes were, to let her stir out for to go round them headlands in an open boat, with such a spell of weather brewing."

"What could ye see of the face of the sky lyin' there?" responded his wife; "it was no fault of your'n; but Neil was daft to go, he was! He might anyway have told Wavie not for to venture it."

"Neil was ever venturesome," sighed Antony. "Ah, well, the child is in God's hands. He saved her once't from the same waves, and He's just as able to do it now. But it's a sore trial, Madge, wife, to stay here in the shelter when that blessed child is out beating against the storm. God grant she may soon come home to us through it all!"

"Amen," said Margaret.

There was a hand laid on the latch, and the blind woman

sprang to her feet; but it was only Owen. The lad came
forward to the fire.

"There's no news of her?" asked Antony.

"Never a word," was the reply. "The night's gettin' main
and dark, so that a body can see nothing. Pat, he says that
Neil would never try for to come roun' Ennis Point in such a
sea as th' yon, but that if he left Miramore at all he'll put in to
shore below Boylah. What d'ye think Antony?"

Antony groaned. "Neil's dreadfully foolhardy, he is! I was
just saying so to Madge afore ye came steppin' in. Neil thinks
no more of risking his life than you'd think of jumping into
the river off the broad stone down yonder. How's the tide? Is
there plenty of water over the bar?"

"Plenty, Antony; I can't be restin' easy here. I will just
go round the shore a bit, towards Boylah; maybe I will see
something of the boat. Pat, and Johndy Bawn, and all the
boys of the town are out along the stran' and over towards
Ennis Point; they cannot rest inside the doors no more nor
I."

"Oh, if only I could be with them!" exclaimed Antony;
"but they'll do all they can, I know."

"There's no fear of them!" said Owen, as he walked to the
door. "There's not a man in Glenderg but who wouldn't cut
off his right hand for Wavie. As for me—I would die for her;
and that's no lie!"

The last sentence was spoken outside, in the dark night;
and there on the hillside, Owen Brennan knelt and prayed
for the safety of the dear companion whose life was in such
peril. Roman Catholic as he was, it was not to saints nor
angels nor even to the Blessed Virgin that he addressed the
petition which came so fervently from his full heart. He felt
instinctively that Wavie must be left to the care of Wavie's
God—the "Father in Heaven" she had so often talked of to
him; and he closed his prayer as Wavie herself would have

done, in the name of the Lord Jesus.

Owen had spoken the truth when he said that none of
the villagers could stay quietly within doors when "the wean"
was in danger. She was no kith nor kin to them, as they
themselves would have expressed it, but there was not one
who did not love her for her sunny smile and winning ways;
even if they had not learned, as Nelly Brennan and her son
had done, the beautiful lessons of Eternal Truth from her
lips, and so loved her for the sake of the words she had read
to them as well as for her own. But with all their willingness,
there was nothing they could do to help her now. The pitchy
darkness foiled all attempts to pierce it, and the howling of
the wind rendered it impossible to distinguish the splash of
oars or the sound of voices: and as for the fury of the raging
sea, no mortal power could master that. No, those in Neil's
boat were beyond all human aid; and the watchers on the
shore knew it right well.

Antony was miserable, doubly so from his forced inaction.
For the first time since his accident, he rose from his bed,
for he felt he could lie still there no longer, listening to the
storm. His wife and Nelly sat by the fire, solacing themselves,
as women will, with dismal recollections of evil past and
yet more dismal forebodings of evil to come. The children
drew forward their little stools and listened, listened to the
talk; and heavy tears filled Madge's twinkling eyes, and little
Dennis forgot his play. Hearts were heavy and anxious in
Glenderg that evening.

And how did it fare with Wavie? She was so accustomed to
the sea that she felt no fear for the first half-hour after leaving
Miramore. The little boat rose bravely over the waves that
came rolling in with terrific height and force; and as the wind
was fair as yet, the rag of sail which they dared to expose was
sufficient to send them rapidly on their way. It was intensely
dark, but the men knew the coast so well that they had no

hesitation as to the course which they ought to pursue.
Wavie, lost in the thoughts of Ada Somerset's kindness and
in speculations as to what Antony and Margaret would do
with the fund of wealth she was bearing home with her,
hardly noticed that each moment the sea rose higher and that
white hissing crests began to show themselves on the tops of
the great billows. After awhile she raised her head, and the
aspect of the water, as it rushed past the side of the boat, not
six inches from her elbow, alarmed her at last. Neil and his
father-in-law stood with ropes in their hands, watching the
effect of each burst of wind and ready to lower the sail at the
first appearance of danger. As far as she could see through the
dusk, the water was broken and white with long foam-tracts
and bubbles—signs, as she well knew, of storms which might
well prove fatal to their frail open boat.

She called aloud in the first sense of her terror. Neil could
not hear her weak voice, through the tumult of the gale; and
even if he had heard, what aid was it in his power to afford?
She gazed around her, and the feeling of powerlessness and
utter desolation came over her—the feeling which has often
chilled the heart and paled the cheek of strong men, when in
like circumstances they realize in all its intensity the nearness
of the death they can do so little to avert. But Wavie, child
as she was, knew who was spoken of in the dear old Bible
at Glenderg as a "hiding place from wind, a covert from
the tempest . . . a place of refuge, a covert from storm and
rain." It was enough! With the remembrance of the words
came back the simple faith which terror had for a moment
overcome; and Wavie, whose call to Neil had been useless
and unheard, now cried to Him whose ear is ever open to the
feeblest utterances of His "little ones," to Him who is "able
to save to the uttermost them who come unto God by Him."
And that merciful Saviour who heard the doubting appeal
of His faithless disciples—"Master, carest Thou not that we

perish?" heard also Wavie's prayer and answered it.

There was a rift in the canopy of clouds, and suddenly the moonlight poured out over the tempestuous scene—showing, with strange shifting effect, the wild grandeur of the ocean. The pale light fell, too, on the cliffs of Ennis Head, stretching across the course the boat was taking, running as they did far into the sea—the huge waves leaping and beating against the solid walls of granite, as the storms of thousands of years had beaten and raged before.

"She'll never make Ennis Head, in the teeth of a sea like—" shouted Neil to the old man; "stand by there! And reef all sail. We'll have to leave the mast a-standing where it is, for it's unpossible to be taking of it down while the boat keeps pitchin' like mad beneath our feet."

"Now for the oars! Try and steady her, while I step astern and lash the rudder so as to shape our course to the south'ard of them black rocks. If there's one inch of groun' . . . Look out, man! Keep her head to it! That big wave was nigh swamping us. May God have mercy on us! . . . If there's one inch of groun' where we can land between this and Glenderg quay, that cove's the place, to this side of them rocks. I know it pretty well, and so do you, for that matter; but it's a risky job."

"Ay, ye may well say so! A risky job, indeed!" muttered the old man. "You're a fool, Neil, and I tould ye so before ever we started. A baby might have know'd that this was no day for crossing to Miramore, let alone—"

But his mutterings and scoldings were unheard; Neil had stepped astern, as he had announced his intention of doing. He changed the lashings of the rudder, and then he looked at Wavie.

"Ye're pretty near frighted to death, so ye are!" he remarked.

She lifted her little face to his in the dim light. "No," she said. "I was frightened awhile ago, but I don't think I am now. I've been thinking of our Saviour when He quieted the sea in just such a bad storm as this is."

But Neil had never heard the story of the fishermen of Gennesaret, and he did not catch the child's meaning.

"The Saviour?" he repeated. "Him as you sing about, 'Exalted on His Throne'? Ay, but what will He trouble about the likes of us? Will He come down to quiet the sea now? Can He quiet such a hurricane as that?" And Neil pointed to where the waves were running in white sheets of broken surge over the low sunken rocks off Carickarn.

"Surely He can," replied the child; "but I think instead of doing it He will save us out of the storm, and that will be better, you see, because I heard you, and Shaw, and Pat Boner saying yesterday that you wanted one more take of leagh this season, and I am sure this gale will bring a plenty in on Glenderg strand."

Not all the finest oratory, not all the expounded doctrine, not all the learning and the eloquence of the whole bench of bishops could have done so much to convince Neil of Christ's power and thoughtful providence as the reply of that little child.

As he bent to his oar, laboring with all his strength to keep the boat from being filled with the water which came in black hissing volumes against her counter, for the first time in his life Neil prayed. And his was not the craven prayer of the coward, face to face with the death he fears, nor the prayer of the sinner who seeks to make a compromise and bargain with heaven; but it was the prayer of the lost sheep, who until then had been so utterly lost that he knew not the voice of the Shepherd, nor the sight of His fold, but who now from the "wilderness out of the way" had caught one glimpse of the distant glory.

Chapter 18
THE TERROR BY NIGHT

"There's no use in calculating to land with dry feet the night," said Neil, as they approached the little cove which lay partly sheltered by the rocks of Carickarn; "and if we try to beach the boat, it's lose her we'll do, sure as a gun."

"It's a pity to lose the boat, bless her!" responded the old man. "The tide is dropping now; it's turned for more than an hour; it's my belief we could beach her well enough, if we hadn't got the wean to look after."

Neil pondered a minute. "Right you are," he said. "We'll pick out the biggest wave we can see and row hard in on its flood. Then as I'm a bit the strongest, I'll jump out and try and drag the boat up every inch I'm able for; and will ye look till the child?"

"Why not let the child sit still where she is? And it's helping you I can be," said the old man.

"Do as I tell ye, and hould yer chatter!" growled his son-in-law. "Nice thing t'would be if the sea should tear the boat from betwixt our fingers, and the child in her! And it's as likely as not we shall find great 'nough to do to

save ourselves, boat or no boat. Wavie!" he shouted in his
stentorian tones, "Wavie! Come up here. Mind how ye step!
Now, mind me. Directly we toss up our oars, you cling fast to
old Connel's neck, and he'll get ye to shore, please God! It's
tryin' to save the boat I'll be; but, by the looks of the job, I
doubt if I'll be man enough to do it."

Poor Wavie had felt an unconquerable repugnance to
Connel at all times. His hard, smoke-dried face, with its
cruel bloodshot eyes, had many a time caused her to shrink
away from him in ill-concealed dislike. It was partly the
consciousness that the child dreaded and avoided him that
caused the old man to regard her with an aversion which
almost amounted to hatred—partly, also, that his half-witted
brain, dull in all but its wickedness, naturally abhorred the
gentle and the pure. He noticed now the shrinking look on
her face, as Neil told her to cling fast to him; and he returned
the look with a smile which was hideous to behold.

"Ye better pitch yer handkerchief of coppers into the sea,"
he said; "I'm thinkin' it will be quite enough to carry yersel',
let alone a poun' weight of yer luggage."

Wavie quietly laid down her bundle of pennies at the
bottom of the boat. "I may keep this, mayn't I?" she asked;
and as she spoke, she innocently held up the green silk purse
which Ada Somerset had given to her, to show how small and
comparatively light it was.

It must have been Satan himself who tempted old Connel
then—tempted him in the darkness and storm; there on
that lonely, desolate shore—tempted him by the sight of the
glittering gold to the crime of robbery and the yet deeper
crime of murder. His soul was black and sin-hardened, yet
even he might have revolted from the brutality of the deed
had he had time for a minute's thought. But the tempter
reckons well his moments of attack, and the idea flashed
into Connel's brain exactly at a time when there could be no

pause for calculation, or consideration of consequences. They were rapidly nearing the cove. Neil was already shouting to him to be ready.

His resolution was taken. The big wave that Neil was watching for, lifted the boat high on its crest—one more powerful stroke of the oars—the signal from Neil, and both men sprang into the surf. Wavie lifted up her bare white arms to him—the trusting action would have melted the hardest heart and turned aside the direst purpose. For one instant Connel wavered—for one instant only; and then his eye caught sight of the fatal purse, clasped in one of those tiny outstretched hands, the faint moonbeams shining upon the treasure contained within its silken meshes. He lifted her from the boat, snatched the purse from her hand, then flung her far from him into the raging sea.

The men struggled through the boiling waters to gain a firm footing on the strand; but the backward rush of the wave had more power than they had counted upon; they reached the shore indeed, but the empty boat floated back on the tide in spite of Neil's strong grasp. And Connel's arms were empty!

"Where's the child?" gasped Neil, his strong voice shaking with emotion.

His father-in-law did not answer, nor did Neil wait for a reply. He rushed to the edge of the advancing wave, searching wildly amongst that waste of tossing, leaping water, for a glimpse of the being who had, almost unknown to himself, awakened the only feelings of affection his callous nature had ever known. He saw his good boat lifted high on the crest of a billow and then hurled at his feet—beaten out of all shape by the power of the sea; but for once Neil was insensible to worldly gain or loss. He was scanning each wave as it neared the shore; was it fancy, or did the moonlight really gleam for an instant on a white, death-like face, and on long tresses of yellow hair? There it was again! Or was it merely a white foam-mass and a tangle of drifting seaweed? Neil watched the wave, as it came rolling on, and then, just as it reared up and curled over to dash itself upon the sand, he dashed in. The water poured over him, beating the breath nearly out of his body; but when the wave had retreated, Neil lay there on the shore, exhausted and bruised indeed, but clasping tightly the inanimate form of the little child who had taught him the name of the Saviour.

He carried her over the moors to Glenderg. It was a long weary way, across morasses, and over barren hills; and the wind blew with unabated fury, though the rain had ceased hours ago. Connel walked a pace or two behind him, lost in remorseful thought. Did Wavie know that he had cast her from him purposely? Would she tell her friends that he had snatched the gold from her hand and flung her into the sea to perish? She lay perfectly still in Neil's arms; perhaps she was already dead.

"The dead tell no tales, they say," thought the wretched old man, as his hand pushed the green silk purse deeper within the folds of his saturated jersey. "What could have possessed Neil to risk his life for the sake of a wean like her; a little white-faced, heretic child of the stranger!"

He wished he had showed Neil the gold, and bid him let the child be, and let the waves work their will with her. Ay, if he had only done that! But then the thought came that in that case he should have had to go shares in the spoil; whereas now it was wholly his own. Yes, it was in fact his own, and he must risk the chance that Wavie knew of his murderous deed and the further chance that if she knew she would ever be able to speak of it.

They reached Glenderg at last, meeting no one, for the people who had gone to seek for them had taken some other way across the dusky mountain. Neil swung himself down the rocks behind the Creigans' cottage, holding the child as tenderly as he could; and Connel slunk away down the pathway to the village.

For the second time, Wavie was borne, drenched and insensible, within the shelter of Antony's home; for the second time, she had been saved from the fury of the storm. She soon recovered consciousness and smiled up into the anxious faces bending over her, telling them not to trouble about her, for she would soon be well. Then a look of suffering swept over the sweet face—suffering so bitter and acute that Nelly Brennan asked her where the pain was and what ailed her.

"Nothing much ails me, I think," she replied; "I have no pain—only I am so tired," and she closed her eyes.

"Go home all on ye," whispered Nelly; "the darlint will do well, please God; least ways none on ye can do her any good." So one by one, with kindly goodnights to the Creigans, and hearty good wishes for Wavie's well-doing, the neighbors departed. She opened her eyes when Neil crossed the earthen floor and put out her hand to him.

"Good-night," she said, "and thank you, Neil."

Neil took the little frail hand in both of his own huge brown ones; he held it for a moment, then laid it gently and reverently down, and turned away without a word.

Chapter 19
ELEANOR'S CHILD

O h, mother dear, I have so much I must tell you," said the child, when no one remained in the cottage excepting their own family and Nelly. "I told the little lady at the big houses all about—"

"Whist ye now, mavourneen," said Antony; "you're not fit to be talkin', sure. Rest ye till the morrow; you're safe and sound at home, thank the Lord! So don't be worriting to tell us aught the night; be aisy and sleep."

But Wavie could not "be easy." She lay back in Margaret's arms, in a strangely nerveless sort of way; then she would start up and cling to her with all her might, while sharp shiverings shook her frame; and the cough which had before alarmed Margaret returned with double strength.

"It's my belief the wean's going to be ill," said the blind woman, under her breath, to Nelly. "Get the childer off to bed; you and me better watch yet awhile."

And watch they did by the side of the child who was so dear to them. Sometimes they thought as they sat there, that they had only received her safe from the dangers of the gloomy night, and stormy sea, to lose her no less surely by other and more gradual means. As the hours passed on, Wavie's feverishness increased to an alarming degree. She started in her sleep, muttering words and broken sentences, which conveyed no meaning to the women who heard her.

"Why don't you save me?" she cried. "Indeed you may have the gold! Oh, don't leave me here in the waves! They are so stormy; they are so cold! Oh, save me, save me, and you shall have the purse. The sea! Oh, save me from the sea!"

"Poor lamb," murmured Margaret, "be at rest. You're safe, my darlint, safe with them who love ye well, safe under the care of the good God, who loves ye, and such as ye, better nor we can do."

She looked up at Margaret's face and smiled.

"Ah, yes," she said, "that is what we have often talked about—'God loves us'—what is it, mother? We were reading about it the other day. Peril, and danger, and death, and the love of God. Oh, what is it? Tell me the words!"

Her voice grew wild and high again as she kept repeating. "Tell me, what is it? Tell me the words."

"Hush, hush! Whist ye, achushla macree[1]!" But it was in vain that the blind woman tried to soothe her.

"Give me the book," said Antony presently. "I think I mind on what she means. We were a-reading it on Sunday mornin'. Take her in-till your arms, wife; and bring her over to this side of the fire, that she may heed me well."

Antony's scanty strength had been almost exhausted by the anxiety he had endured all that terrible evening; and his fingers, white and thin now, trembled as he turned over the leaves of the Bible. A mark had been placed in St. Paul's Epistle to the Romans, where Wavie had last been reading to him, and he soon turned to the verses which he fancied she must mean. They were these:

---

1   *pulse of my heart*

"If God be for us, who can be against us?

"He that spared not His own Son, but delivered Him up for us all, how shall He not with Him also freely give us all things?

"Who shall separate us from the love of Christ? Shall tribulation, or distress, or persecution, or famine, or nakedness, or peril, or sword?

"Nay, in all these things we are more than conquerors through Him that loved us.

"For I am persuaded that neither death, nor life, nor angels, nor principalities, nor powers, nor things present, nor things to come,

"Nor height, nor depth, nor any other creature, shall be able to separate us from the love of God, which is in Christ Jesus our Lord."

Antony Creigan's voice shook as he read, slowly and hesitatingly, those wonderful words. The wind still swept in fierce gusts around the hills, the sea still sobbed upon the shore, but Wavie was asleep.

∞

The morrow came, and a travelling carriage, with post horses, the best which could be hired at Miramore, set out on the long mountain journey to Glenderg. Mrs. Somerset had written to Colonel Buchanan, while Ada was eating her breakfast. She herself could touch nothing, although her maid Elizabeth urged upon her the necessity of keeping up what strength she had got; so the servant consoled herself by packing into a hamper enough wine and eatables to have lasted treble the length of time her mistress expected to be away.

As they drove northward, Ada could scarcely control her impatience. When the horses crawled slowly up the steep

hills, she knelt on the seat and looked impatiently through
the front windows, wondering why they could not walk
faster; or she peered out to see if she could perceive the top
of the ascent. Along the small tracts of level ground, and
down the slopes and pitches, the pace which the Miramore
coachman considered sufficiently swift, appeared to her as
most tantalisingly slow and loitering. She appealed sometimes
to her grandmother to urge him to drive faster, but Mrs.
Somerset only bade her sit still and did not even smile at the
little girl's impetuosity.

They inquired sometimes at the hamlets they passed
which was the nearest way to the place where the Queen of
the Wave had been wrecked, three years ago. But in Ireland
it is a matter of great difficulty to squeeze lucid directions
concerning roads, or correct definitions of distance, out of
the inhabitants of the more remote districts. Several times
the carriage took a wrong turning, and many steps had to be
retraced. It was late in the afternoon when Glenderg was at
last reached, and Mrs. Somerset beckoned with her hand to a
lad who was passing at the moment.

"Can you tell me where a little girl is living, named Agatha
Buchanan?" she asked him. "She was rescued from the wreck
of the ship Queen."

"It will be our Wavie ye mean, ma'am," said Owen, for
he it was, startled out of his good manners to the extent of
interrupting the lady.

"Oh, yes, yes!" exclaimed Ada, "that is it; she is called
Wavie here; she told me so. Where is she?"

"Ye've come a few steps past the turning to the house,"
replied Owen; "she lives at Anton's, over against the brae
there. I'm a'going up now mysel' to see how she is; she's
terrible bad, they do say."

"Bad!"

"Yes, she was nigh drownded coming from Miramore last

night. Fools that we all were till let the likes of her go at all!" said the boy, between his white even teeth.

Mrs. Somerset was paler than ever when she stepped from the carriage, and Ada walked quite silently by her side as, guided by Owen, they ascended the pathway leading to the Creigans' cottage.

Owen was lost in wonderment. Here were Wavie's grand relations come at last, come to take her away from Glenderg, and from him. What should he do without her? What would his life be without the sweet little companion who had made so much of life's sunshine for him? He knew he ought to be glad for her sake; but somehow the consciousness of his selfishness, if selfishness it was, did not make the thought of losing her easier to be borne. He followed behind, gazing, as though he saw it not, at Mrs. Somerset's purple silk, the richness of color and texture of which at any other time would have excited his marvelling admiration.

Nelly Brennan was standing at the cottage door; Owen stepped forward.

"Mother," he said, "these be our Wavie's friends come for her to find her at long last."

Nelly curtseyed, but Mrs. Somerset, hardly hearing the rude attempt at introduction, or noticing the peasant woman at all, brushed past her into the cottage.

"Where is she?" she asked hurriedly.

Nelly, considerably hurt at the lady's manner, followed her and took up a position between the intruder and the door of the inner room.

"Where is the child?" said Mrs. Somerset again, and looking around as she spoke.

Antony half raised himself on his pillow as the lady's eyes fell on him and pointed to the door of the room. "It's in there she is, ma'am," he said; "but she's sore and ill—God save us!"

"'Deed, and you're not goin' to her!" said Nelly firmly, as
Mrs. Somerset advanced. "The doctor's with her now, and
moreover she's off her head already, and the sight of strangers
might send her off clean, forever."

Mrs. Somerset was amazed. She was not accustomed to
have her will disputed, or her movements thwarted by any
one; and the fact of this woman, with her tattered dress,
and half intelligible English, attempting to do so, was almost
incredible.

"Nelly," said Antony, beginning to expostulate.

But further parley was cut short by the opening of the
door behind the widow Brennan, and Dr. Doran came
forward. The lady appealed to him at once. She told him
who she was and explained that it had only been yesterday
that she had the faintest idea that her granddaughter might
have survived the wreck of the ship, but that she had come
immediately to take her away.

"I regret to say, madam, that that is impossible," said the
doctor. "I fear the child will have a sharp attack of brain fever,
brought on by excessive excitement; and there is threatened
danger of inflammation of the lungs. Her constitution is an
exceedingly delicate one, and in her present state it would
be madness to attempt to remove her. She is indeed most
alarmingly ill."

Little Ada gave half a sob. All the dignity and ruffled
feeling departed from Mrs. Somerset's manner, and she
clasped her hands together with a gesture which had
something in it of the anguish she had endured the night
before.

"But how can she remain in this—place?" she said,
supplying the last word instead of the less complimentary one
which was on her lips, out of regard to Antony, who of course
could hear everything that passed.

"She is quite comfortable here; she is used to it, you must

remember," said the doctor in a low tone; "besides, if she were in a palace it could make but little difference to her now."

"I may see her?"

"Surely," and Dr. Doran led the way to Wavie's bedside.

She was lying back upon her pillow, her blue eyes bright with the fever which was upon her, her golden hair tossed off in a tangled heap from her forehead, which was flushed and hot, and her little hands beating the coverlet in the restlessness of delirium. Margaret was bending over the bed. She raised herself and came forward, as her quick ear remarked the strange footstep and the unwonted rustle of silken attire. Dr. Doran drew her aside to explain, and Mrs. Somerset took her place by Wavie's side. Her daughter's child! And this was how she had found her!

Ada had followed her grandmother, and at the sight of the cousin she had all that day so longed to reach, lying there with that strange wild look in her eye, she sobbed aloud, "O Wavie, Wavie!"

The sound seemed to disturb her and to pierce even to her fever-struck brain.

"Don't cry," she said; "it was God who let him throw me into the sea. Don't cry about it so. Don't you remember—

'Here we suffer grief and pain,
Here we meet to part again
In heaven we part no more!'

"I forget the rest—Neil knows it; I've sung it to him so often. But I cannot now. Oh, the sea! The sea!"

Again the paroxysm of delirium came over her, and she clung to Margaret, screaming and trembling.

"What does she mean about the sea?" asked Mrs. Somerset in a low, broken tone.

"It was a fearsome storm last night, ma'am, and they a'most lost their lives comin' across the bay. The boat hersel' was smashed, and it was all that Neil and Connel could do to save theirsel's and her."

"My poor darling!" murmured the lady softly. "My poor darling! Exposed to all this danger and terror, when you would have been shielded from every rough wind, from every rude hand, if only I had not been so neglectful and inert. You must live, Agatha, if only to say you forgive me, and for me to prove how I can love you, my Eleanor's child."

Chapter 20
COLONEL BUCHANAN

D r. Doran really pitied Mrs. Somerset. She was so
completely out of her element in the Creigans' cottage.
Her passionate love for her lost Eleanor seemed to awake
again in all its intensity to be lavished on her little daughter,
who, in the good doctor's opinion, was rapidly approaching
the gates of death. There seemed much difficulty in
knowing what course to be taken in arranging matters. The
idea of removing Wavie was abandoned the moment her
grandmother saw with her own eyes the condition she was in.
What was to be done? Mrs. Somerset could not find it in her
heart to leave her and return with Ada to Miramore. Yet to
remain at Glenderg seemed impossible.

The earthen floor, the brown rafters, the scanty
furniture—altogether made up a picture such as she had
never before realized. She was not a selfish woman and
would have cheerfully endured actual pain or made
great sacrifices for those she loved; but putting her own
convenience utterly aside, it seemed that for her to remain
in such a place was out of the question. And if it was so bad

for her to endure, what must it be for the sufferer? It was hard to believe there could be a chance for her life there in that squalid place, tended by a blind woman and an old wretch who could scarcely speak English, for so the lady mentally designated Nelly Brennan, who had found no favor in her eyes.

Dr. Doran felt all these things and pondered over them for a minute or two; then he approached Mrs. Somerset.

"Oh, what must I do?" said the lady appealing to him in her perplexity. "I cannot remain here for the night—Ada too—and it is not possible to return to Miramore today—it is getting dark already!—even supposing I could bring myself to leave this dear child here for an hour by herself, now that I know she is my own flesh and blood. Is there any place near, any hotel or lodging house, where I can go?"

Dr. Doran shook his head. "No," he replied; "this is a wild region; there is nothing I can suggest except this—my house is about six miles from here, in 'the town' as it is termed, near the little church, which you may have remarked as you came. If you would accept the very humble hospitality which my wife and I can offer you, I shall be pleased to place our one spare room at your disposal. You could be here again early tomorrow and make any arrangements which might seem fit to you; but as long as you will honor me by remaining under my roof, I shall be—"

Mrs. Somerset interrupted his hesitation by expressing her gratitude very warmly. She could not see any other or more feasible plan, and she accepted the doctor's courtesy, recognizing the true kindness which prompted it. So she pressed many kisses on Agatha's flushed forehead, said all she could say of acknowledgment and thanks to the wonderstruck Antony and Margaret, and let Dr. Doran lead her down to the carriage.

"I shall send to Miramore for every obtainable

convenience and luxury," she said, as they walked down the
pathway; "and would it be well to have my maid—who is a
most sensible, trustworthy person—to assist in the nursing?"

"Oh, no, certainly not!" said Dr. Doran warmly; and
then he added, as if in apology for his manner, "You see,
madam, the Creigans have proved themselves such real and
true friends to the child; they have loved her so fondly, and
generously; they would be hurt now by any appearance of
doubt. Your own claim of course they can acknowledge; but
they would not like to see your maid waiting on her, nor
indeed do I suppose that she herself would understand my
friends Antony and his wife."

Perhaps the slight accent of reproach in his tone was not
lost upon Mrs. Somerset. She was very silent as they drove
away.

Ada's face was sad and tearful. She, poor child, left
Miramore with very different feelings from those with
which she had approached the place. Her anticipation of
the pleasure of Wavie's companionship had been full of
delight: "a real sister she would be, such as other girls had."
But instead of this, she could only carry away with her the
remembrance of that fever-flushed face and of those brilliant
eyes, which had flashed across her own with no gleam of
recognition. It seemed very sudden, very terrible, to Ada. It
was her first lesson in that truth which is ever so difficult to
learn, that God's ways are not our ways, nor His thoughts as
our thoughts.

For many days Wavie lay at death's door. Dr. Doran, and
the physician they had sent for from Miramore, gave little
or no hope of her recovery. She had too small a share of
strength, they said, to withstand the ravages of the fever; and
then there was that deeper mischief still—the inflammatory
symptoms about the lungs. A short time more would decide;
in a day or two, at the furthest, the crisis would arrive.

Mrs. Somerset went to Glenderg every morning and did all that it was in her power to do for the child's comfort. Everything that money or effort could procure was lavishly provided, but it made little or no difference to Wavie. Consciousness had not returned to her, and sometimes her grandmother feared she would pass away from earth without ever knowing that her relatives had found her at last, and that nearer, if not dearer, friends stood round the sick bed than those she had known before.

Would Colonel Buchanan never come? No answer had arrived to the letter which Mrs. Somerset had written from Miramore; and she had sent a second, and a third, telling him of the state in which she had found the little Agatha; but still there was no word of or from him.

It was Sunday morning—a grey cold day; and Mrs. Somerset and Ada, accompanied by Mrs. Doran, a shy, gentle, delicate little woman, were leaving the doorsteps of the doctor's house on their way to church, when an Irish car, with a pair of horses, harnessed tandem fashion, came rapidly down "the street," as the broad roadway, with its few straggling houses on either side, was generally termed.

As the vehicle was passing them, a deep voice suddenly called to the driver to stop, and a gentleman sprang to the ground and approached them. Mrs. Somerset recognized him instantly. It was Agatha's father, come at last.

"Where is she? Am I too late?" he said, as he grasped her offered hand. "Is this Glenderg?"

Mrs. Somerset explained why it was she was there and told him of the extreme danger in which they believed the child lay. Colonel Buchanan was evidently a man of few words; he listened to her attentively, and then he said, "I shall go on immediately; goodbye."

"I intended to go myself this afternoon," she responded, "but I can accompany you now."

"No," he said, "pray do not. I received all your letters together, for I was out of town for a day or two when they arrived, but I have travelled night and day since, and really what with anxiety and some share of fatigue; I am no fit society for any one." He smiled as he spoke, such a smile as makes a face sadder rather than brighter, and then he mounted into his seat again and drove off.

How altered he was! Mrs. Somerset thought; and she was right. The stalwart, handsome young officer who had taken her Eleanor from her side could hardly be traced in the grey-haired, grave-faced man who had just left her. But there was a difference far greater than any of mere outward appearance—a difference of which the eye of God alone could see the magnitude. The selfish, godless, careless nature was changed into humble-hearted hopefulness and charity—the heart that had wandered far among mists and doubts had passed into sunshine at last, had looked up from the things of time and earth, and had found that God the Avenger, God the Judge, is also God the Father, the God of love.

The Creigans knew that Mrs. Somerset daily expected Colonel Buchanan to arrive from England, therefore they guessed at once who the tall gentleman must be who came striding up the hill at such a rapid pace. Margaret went to the door. "You're welcome, sir," she said, when she knew by the sound of his footsteps that her visitor had almost reached her. "You're welcome, but it's ill news you have to learn."

He removed his hat with a gesture as courteous as if he were addressing a duchess. "I know it," he said, "but I thank God I have arrived in time."

Antony was sitting by the fire; he rose to his feet as Colonel Buchanan entered, but he was too weak to advance even a single step. It was Owen who led the father into the inner room and drew back the shawl which hung over the small window, that he might look upon his child; and then with the instinctive delicacy so often found in the Irish peasant's character, he withdrew and left them alone together.

It was nearly an hour before the door opened again. "I have kept you a long time from your patient," he said to Margaret. "Have the doctors seen her today?"

"Yes, yer honor," replied Antony, as his wife went to Wavie's bedside. "Both on them have been here the day, and Dr. Doran comes again this evenin' with the lady. Ye'll wait and see him?" questioned Antony, supposing that, as Mrs. Somerset had not remained there, Colonel Buchanan would not do so either.

"Surely," he replied. "I don't intend to leave my child again; that is, if you will allow me to stay here? There! There! Don't say a word about accommodation and all that sort of thing. I am a soldier, Creigan, and can manage to be comfortable anywhere. I will speak about it to your wife."

He re-entered the room where Margaret was now laying cold-water bandages on Wavie's brow. He stood silently by, while the blind woman's dexterous fingers soothed his little daughter's pain; he watched her face full of gentlest love; he saw her sightless eyes suffused with tears; and he heard the caressing words which she murmured—words which sounded soft and tender, though they were in the strange old Erse tongue which he had never heard before.

He came close beside her and spoke almost in a whisper, with utterance choked by his intense feeling.

"I have to thank you, Mrs. Creigan, for your goodness and great love to my child. I pray God she may live to thank you, too."

"You've naught to thank us for, sir; she's fully as dear to us as one of our own. She's been a blessin' to us, sir, such as we can never tell about, for lack of words to say it in. She has been sight to me, sir, since I lost my eyesight; she has teached the childer their bits of lessons; and since Antony

was 'most killed by the fall of the roof—as yer honor sees—she
has nursed him and read till him; and she has gone times and
times to Miramore to sell winkles, and such like, which she
and the childer catched on the shore. Ah, sir, what we'll do
without her I cannot tell—and I fear me we're boun' to lose
her, whether she lives or dies. She's knit to our hearts with
cords which can never, never break."

Every word Margaret spoke struck like an arrow to Colonel
Buchanan's heart. This, then, was the just punishment for
his neglect of the trust given him by God and left him by
his dying wife. He had given over his duty into other hands,
carelessly and lightly; and now when he would sacrifice long
years of his life to be able to atone to his little daughter
for his lack of love and care, he hears of her existence only
to find her lying there, sick almost unto death—that voice
which had never called him "father" moaning out her pain,
or raised with all the wildness of delirium. And now he
hears the humble peasant woman—to whom she had been
indebted for shelter and for bread—telling of her sweetness
and gentleness—telling of it to him, her father—who knew
less of her than did the rough-headed lad who stood leaning
against the wall, gazing at her with a world of affection in his
sad eyes.

Chapter 21
THE VALLEY OF THE SHADOW

All who were near the bedside of the child knew full well that the doctors had spoken truth and that she must die. Mrs. Somerset thought each time she passed from her little room that she had taken her last look at the little sufferer's living face—and that the next time she should enter there would be to find that the Shadow which had been resting over the cottage had fallen at last.

Colonel Buchanan knew that all his devotion, all his care and love, would be in vain. He knew it as he listened to Agatha's ravings, when the fever ran high. He heard her sayings—in the midst of her terror at the haunting remembrances of waves and storm—that she knew her Father in Heaven was taking charge of her and that she was wrong to be afraid. He heard her trusting prayers for help and guidance; and as he listened, he felt that a spirit so self-forgetful, so beautiful, in trustfulness and purity, was more fit to be "safely garnered" above, than to sojourn long on earth, amidst trials and crosses and sin.

He learned all the simple tale of this little daughter's

life, as he watched by her during those nights and days. He heard also of the crime which Connel had committed; and the hot blood rose in his cheek, and his teeth gnawed the ends of his long moustache as he heard.

In her unconscious utterances and moanings, she revealed all and lived over again the horrors of the moment when she had been tossed by the old man's wicked hands, back into the seething sea. She clung tightly to her father's arms, piteously entreating him not to be so cruel, not to leave her there to die! And then—all the terror passing away from her face—she would say in her usual gentle voice: "It is the Saviour's will! I told you, Neil, He would manage all for the best; and so I am certain sure He *will*! Tell them all at home, Neil, that He will find them money some other way, when I'm not here any more to try and earn pennies for them."

If Colonel Buchanan learnt all Wavie's love for her friends from her own lips, he learned from the actions which speak more eloquently than words of all the depth of their love for her. And he could see also what she had been to the fisher-folk who crowded to the door each night and morning for news of her. Rough men returning from their daily work in the fields, or on the shore, would walk round by way of Antony's cottage to hear how the "dear lassie was now." The children would hush their noisy play and bring great armfuls of purple heather and golden gorse, saying that "Wavie always loved the flowers."

Neil's dark face was often to be seen peering into the cabin, and sometimes he begged to be allowed "just one sight of the child." Colonel Buchanan shrank from the man; he had an evil look, he thought; and if he was not the ruffian who had tried to murder his daughter, at least he was there at the time and might have been in league with him; for all that, events proved to the contrary. He did not

know—for Wavie herself did not know—that Neil had risked
his own life to save hers and that he would gladly have done
it again a dozen times over, for she was the only thing in all
the world that the hard man cared for—the only thing he
reverenced—and it sometimes seemed to him she was the
only link that, frail as it was, united him to goodness, and
the "Saviour."

Owen was miserable. The sole consolation he could find
was in being continually at Colonel Buchanan's beck and
call. He would walk miles to the post office for his letters.
He had ridden twice all the way to Miramore on the black
pony—gladly lent by Michael—with a message to the doctor
there. He waited on the gentleman with an untiring zeal,
which would have roused the Colonel's wonder, had he
not been too absorbed with his child to notice it much.
Owen tried hard to realize, what he had once preached to
Wavie when she was in sore distress, that "all things work
together for good to them that love God." He *had* tried
in his ignorant way to love Him, yet this thing could not
work for his good any way, he thought. Who was to read to
him when Wavie was gone? How was he ever to join her in
heaven, he a poor wretched fisher boy, with no learning or
knowledge about anything? For he, too, felt that she would
die; and then, what remained for him?

Margaret was too busy to grieve as Owen did.
Notwithstanding her blindness, she waited on Wavie
continually; and there was Antony to care for and Madge
and little Dennis to mind—though it was true the poor
children did not need much cautioning to hush their
noisy games and to keep the house as still as might be. Her
husband still suffered from pain and weakness, but his
patience, and even his cheerfulness, never failed him.

When Colonel Buchanan felt he could look no longer
on his child's sufferings, he would go from her sick bed

to Antony's side and listen to his talk of Wavie, with an
interest which never flagged. It puzzled him, as he sat
listening there, how it could be that this poor man who
knew so little, whose life had been so humble, and so mean,
could yet have learnt a code of honor as keen as his own.
It puzzled him to hear from Antony Creigan's lips noble,
high-souled words, words of courage and hope, when there
was so much to have bidden him despair. It puzzled him
until he saw in the man evidences of a faith too confiding
and single-hearted to bear the suspicion of "cant"; a faith
which Colonel Buchanan, who had mingled with the
learned and well-born, had never known surpassed.

The gentleman thus strangely domiciled in the cottage in
the wild mountains of Donegal was a different being from
the silent, dignified man, whom his brother officers had
deemed cold and proud. His daughter's friends had become
his friends, in a sense which his equals in rank and fortune
had not been, since the days when he went with Harry
Somerset to spend his furlough in the quiet old English
town where he had first met his wife. How long ago those
Aylchester days appeared to him now! Yet he seemed nearer
to Eleanor than he had done since the earth was closed over
her Canadian grave. The hope had dawned long since of
rejoining her in the land where, as Wavie's hymn phrased it,
"We meet to part no more." But now the distance between
them was bridged over. Their little child was about to pass
from his arms to hers. The outer world, with its bustle and
its stir, was shut off from him behind the blue hills, and
heaven seemed near to the cottage where Agatha lay dying
and where Antony Creigan's voice could repeat firmly and
joyfully: "In all these things we are more than conquerors
through Him that loved us!"

Late on Friday afternoon, the Colonel went out on the
strand for a breath of fresh air. He had left Wavie sleeping

and Margaret sitting by her side. Mrs. Somerset and Ada had paid their daily visit and had heard Dr. Doran's opinion, which had varied little for many days past. The dreary sense of waiting pressed upon him. He knew full well that it could not be very long before the ties which held him to Glenderg would be snapped; and though he shrank from clothing that knowledge in words, or even from letting it take definite shape in his thoughts, yet it was none the less certainly there. The day was in itself dreary. It was close on November now, and the sunlight and warmth of the late Donegal summer had vanished. The grey waves came from under the grey sky in slowly moving rollers; and far out in the west, where the low horizon stooped to the water, there was a dark inky line which foretold bad weather. The scene was hardly inviting enough to keep a mere idler upon the shore from choice, but it chimed in with Colonel Buchanan's mood; and as he paced along the edge of the waves, he thought of his earthly pilgrimage, stretching out, dim and unknown before him—the past, with more of sorrow and sin to mark it than of good, and the future, grey and cold, as far as he could discern it, like yonder sea. He could have echoed the words of the patriarch Jacob: "Few and evil have the days of the years of my life been." Yet he knew now that the hand which had guided him from his wanderings "in the wilderness, out of the way," would lead him unto the end.

Little Madge came towards him, her bare feet gleaming as she sped across the sand, her tangled elf-locks blown out upon the breeze.

"Oh please, sir," she panted, "mother sent me to tell ye that Wavie is hersel' again. She waked up quite as she used to be afore she got ill."

"Thank the Lord!" said Colonel Buchanan, very low. And he began to walk hurriedly towards the house.

"Please, sir," said little Madge, lifting her wide-open eyes to his face, "sure Wavie'll soon be well again now! Won't she?"

"I cannot tell," he answered her. "It must be as God sees best."

"It must be best, then for her to get well. I know it must! Ah, but we've missed her sore! Dennis and me."

Chapter 22
FORGIVENESS

"Indeed it is better so, papa, if only you could think it."
The fierce fever had left her entirely; the crisis the doctors had spoken of had come and gone, and they said that probably it would take but very few days for the remainder of her faint strength to ebb away. There was no need to break the news to Wavie. She knew it quite well already; and lying in her father's arms, her head pillowed on his broad shoulder, she repeated: "Indeed it is best so, papa."

She had listened to the tale he had told her with a quiet sense of comprehension. It did not seem to astonish or bewilder her. The child had got beyond the dazzling and distorting atmosphere of earth, into the clearer light which beams out from the gates of the Father's kingdom, and in that light earthly things appear strangely different. She had received her grandmother's caresses as if she had known her all her brief life; and it was only when Ada began to talk of the future, when she should have Wavie with her in her old haunts in Aylchester, that the sweet face became troubled, and the beautiful eyes looked distressfully round for her father. With him she seemed at ease at once. It appeared so natural to her to be lifted in his firm clasp and to hear the tender tones of his deep voice.

"But, Wavie," he answered (he had almost unawares adopted the name first given her by the lisping Dennis), "but, Wavie, how can it be best so, when I shall be left alone in the world? I have no one but you to care for, no one but you on earth to care much for me. I cannot spare you, Wavie!"

"Yes, papa, you can—far better than if I had always been with you. You will have to live for many years, ordering all your soldiers and . . . and doing plenty of other things; and if ever you are lonely, you must think of our Saviour, and of mamma, and me, waiting for you in the land we read about in the big Bible yonder. But—"

"But what, my child?"

"They will miss me so much here, papa. You know that father—I mean father Antony—will not be able to work for a long time to come; and poor mother is blind and can't do very much. I had such hopes of helping them, and now—"

"They shall not want for anything whilst they live, Wavie; you may be certain of that."

She smiled. "Thank you, papa. I was sure that you and the lady (she had never given Mrs. Somerset any other title) would be good to them; but still I'm afraid they will miss me when I am gone.

"There's Owen, too," she went on, after a pause. "He cried so today when I was talking about it. Poor Owen! I never saw him cry before."

"I think I shall take Owen back to England with me, my darling; that is, provided he likes to come. I will train him, and care for him, and do all I can for him, for the sake of the love he bears my daughter. Nelly can live up here with the Creigans and help Margaret. I fancy Owen will like that plan and will be glad to come with me after—" He stopped suddenly and gathered the fragile little form closer into his embrace.

Yet Wavie finished the sentence in the calm, even tone in which she had spoken before.

"After I am gone. Yes, Owen will be sure to like that. He likes you so much, papa; he says you are such a brave, noble gentleman; and I think so too! It is so pleasant to know you like this, because, you see, mamma and I shall have plenty to talk about now; and if I had never even seen you I should have been like a stranger to her."

Colonel Buchanan did not reply. Since the day he had stood by his wife's coffin, he had never once spoken of her. In the sad time which followed her death, they had come to him for directions and had asked to know his wishes concerning her funeral—and for his directions about the usual gloomy surroundings of death and the grave. But he had answered impatiently that they might do as they chose and had bidden them not to worry him, for what difference could anything in all the wide world make to her now? He had walked in the place they assigned to him in the funeral cortége with a stony look on his set face. Immediately afterwards he had left his brother's house and returned to his duties at the garrison; there, none of his brother officers dared to speak to him of his loss; and Eleanor's name had never passed his lips—until he bent over his daughter's dying bed.

It appeared passing strange to him to hear the child talking in that quiet, real fashion of her approaching meeting with the mother she had never known. He sat there, silently, in the little room, with its earthen floor and smoke-stained rafters—the evening light streaming in through the tiny squares of glass which formed the window and resting on Wavie's head, until her hair shone like an aureole of glory above her blue-veined brow. She raised herself higher on his shoulder.

"Papa," she whispered, "we shall watch for you at the gate, mamma and I; and it won't seem very long to wait, for time must pass quickly in heaven."

"But, my darling, what if I am not worthy to come? What if you watch in vain?"

"Oh, papa!" and the distress in her voice was so acute that Colonel Buchanan regretted that he had suggested the doubt. "Oh, papa, you must come! It does not matter the very least about being 'worthy,' for I remember reading in our Bible: 'Not by works of righteousness which we have done, but according to Christ's mercy, He saves us.' So you will come, dear, dear, papa! Will you not?"

There was a short pause; her eyes were fixed on his face with an imploring look which went to his heart. The momentary faithlessness passed from him. "Christ's mercy!" Was it not enough to trust to? He bent his head until his lips touched her forehead, and he answered her slowly and solemnly: "Yes, my child; God helping me, I will come."

∞

That same evening, long after the sun had set behind the western clouds, a man might have been seen coming with hesitating steps towards Antony's cabin. He did not approach by the usual path, up the hill from the shore; but he came across the moor on the heights above. The door stood ajar, and he looked in cautiously. Antony was sitting on the hearth in an invalid chair, one of the many things which had been brought at the Colonel's orders from Londonderry, and which was a marvel of cushioned comfort in the eyes of the whole household. Margaret's nimble fingers were plying her glistening knitting needles by his side. The two children were playing with a bundle of rushes on the floor; and Owen sat near, on a low stool, his chin on his hands and his elbows resting on his knees. The door of the room was half open, and the soft glow of the Colonel's reading lamp shone from it.

An involuntary sound betrayed the intruder's presence. Antony looked up and recognized the outline of his figure.

"Step in, Connel," he said, beneath his breath; "but be as aisy as you can, man, will ye? She's sleepin' a bit, God bless her!"

Some powerful attraction for which he could not account, but which it was impossible for him to resist, had drawn the guilty Connel to the cottage where Wavie was lying. He had not intended to enter, but he advanced a step or two, making some commonplace reply to Antony's invitation. His voice, few as his words were, reached the inner room and roused the sleeping child as surely as a trumpet note would have done. She started up on her pillow, listening eagerly.

"My darling! What is it?" asked her father.

"Papa, there is Connel out there—a man I want to speak to, please. May he come in? And, papa, would you mind very much if he was to be here quite alone? I want to say something to him which—which—" and she hesitated.

"Wavie, I know what you mean. I know what Connel did, or tried to do."

"Papa! Who told you?"

"You did, in your ravings. My darling, I heard it all—all your terror—all the bitterness of death which you tasted at that villain's hands! Oh, Wavie, do not see him again! You are not strong enough to bear it. Besides—"

"I must see him," repeated the child, wearily; and her face was quite calm and quiet. Her father gazed at her for a minute silently; at last he said:

"If I bring him in, you must let me stay," and then Colonel Buchanan, not knowing how to refuse her, yet dreading to allow the excitement he feared would ensue, stepped into the kitchen and returned with the unwilling Connel.

Wavie held out her hand to him: that same little hand she had stretched out towards him over the side of Neil's boat.

Connel shrank back, as if those tiny fingers had dealt him a heavy blow. He glanced at the door and would have escaped, but the Colonel's grasp upon his shoulder held him firmly.

"I wanted to tell you, Connel," said Wavie, in her sweet tones, "to tell you that I quite forgive you for leaving me in the sea. I thought that perhaps you might be sorry sometime, and it would comfort you then to know that I, and papa, quite forgive you. I am sure you may keep that money for your very own. Goodbye."

The dazed look of abject fear which rested on the old man's cunning face changed to one of astonishment, and then to a softness and a sorrow such as it had never worn before. He would have fallen on his knees; he would have spoken to her; he would have cried out in his repentance and his contrition; but the Colonel's iron grip drew him out of the room, through the kitchen, and into the open air. He would have hurled him away and bid him begone, caitiff, murderer as he was, but the remembrance of the words, "I, and papa, quite forgive you," restrained all outward evidence of the anger which was raging within him. He took his hand from Connel's collar and pointed down the road. "Go," he said, "and pray that God may forgive you, as that angel child has done!"

Chapter 23
THE GLORIOUS HOME

I should like to see the lady again, and Ada, papa," said Wavie, awakening from one of the death-like slumbers which followed one another at brief intervals all through that night.

"You shall see them tomorrow, dearest," said Colonel Buchanan, bending over her and passing his handkerchief over her damp brow.

"Tomorrow, papa, I shall be gone. Please tell them I should have liked to have bid them, 'Goodbye,' for they have been very kind to me. You won't forget?"

"No, my darling, I won't forget. I shall forget nothing you have ever said to me, my own child."

Alas, he had not very much to remember, only three short days of converse with that sweet spirit, who had already passed within sight of the shores of heaven.

"Thank you," and she stroked his hand with her cold fingers. "Mother, dear," she said presently, to Margaret, who was kneeling beside her, "you must all be very happy when I'm gone; you will miss me at first, I know—but you must be

glad for me, too. Papa will take care that you have plenty of
pennies—more than ever I could have earned—and so there
won't be any more need for you to fret about things."

Antony came slowly across the floor; he was very feeble
still. She smiled as she caught his look and said: "You will
think of me when you read about the great multitude in the
Psalms and the robes washed white, will you not? I am sure
my Saviour will send for me soon, and I shall be glad to go.
I should only grieve Him by sinfulness if I stayed here; so
I shall be glad to go to Him now, though I love you all so
much, so very much!"

No one answered her; they had no power to speak just
then. After a minute the blue eyes again unclosed, and she
said, "Owen!"

"I am here," replied the poor boy, his voice hoarse with
weeping.

"You will keep with papa always, Owen? I wish you would
tell him what you bade me remember the day father was hurt,
about all things working together for good. And tell him
about all we used to talk of and all we did. I have not had
time to tell him much, you see; and he would like to hear it
all, I know . . . I am so tired, now, papa; lift me up in your
arms, and I shall go to sleep."

Colonel Buchanan did as she bade him; he lifted her
from her little low bed and wrapped around her some soft
chinchilla furs of Mrs. Somerset's. She slept more softly and
peacefully then than she had done since the sickness had first
seized upon her. Her father held her closely and shuddered
as he marked the cold grey shadow, which crept up over her
face. One hour after another passed by, but they did not
speak nor move. The two children slumbered on their pallet
on the other side of the room. The peat fire burned lower
and lower, soft white ashes gathering around the glowing
center of living fire. The night had passed into that darkest

hour which precedes the dawn, and still they watched her sleeping there.

Suddenly she opened her eyes and spoke; and her voice rang sweet and clear, as those who were gathered around her had often heard it ring out over the breezy moors, or along the stretch of the shore.

"Oh, look!" she said, "it is the morning!" She threw up her hands. A smile broke over her face—a smile of inexpressible beauty, and brightness, and joy. There was one long-drawn, gentle sigh, and with the sigh the spirit fled.

There was silence for awhile, and then Antony repeated: "Death is swallowed up in victory. O Death, where is thy sting? O Grave, where is thy victory? Thanks be to God, who giveth us the victory, through Jesus Christ our Lord."

∾

"You will not allow her to be buried here in this horrible, desolate place," said Mrs. Somerset to her son-in-law. "Do give orders for her to lie with her ancestors in our own family vault."

"As you please," Colonel Buchanan answered. "It will make no difference to me; it shall be as you desire."

But his reply, although alike in words, was very different in spirit to the one he had given when they had asked him where his wife should be laid. Then his heart was full of bitterness; his idol was shattered, and he cared not what became of its shrine. Then he had mourned as one that had lost his all—he had braved Fate's cruellest arrow—he had outlived life's heaviest grief, and he cared little either for present or future.

Now all was changed. He knew his wife and his child were his still—waiting for him at the Gates of the "Glorious City"—and he had promised, God helping him, to meet them

there. Mrs. Somerset might do as she pleased with the little
corpse which lay, in its sweet childish beauty, in the humble
home she had made radiant by her presence in life. It was
not his Wavie. He did not even cut off one of the long golden
tresses, which lay across the pillow. No, he felt that his child
had no more to do with earth; she was—as Owen had said to
him—"Yonder."

A day or two afterwards, Colonel Buchanan grasped
Antony's wasted hand in both his own. "Farewell, my friend.
We shall meet again. I have never thanked you for your love,
and for your kindness to her, because I could not do so if I
were to try. God bless you, and yours. And, Antony, when you
speak to God, here in your cottage, sometimes remember to
pray for me, that I may indeed remain faithful unto the end."

So he left them; Owen following his steps.

∽

The winter set in, severe and cold, and the waves
thundered along the strand. Then the springtime came;
and the tender grass blades lifted their tiny spears from the
ground, to shiver in the cold east wind. But in the month of
May, the east winds were all over, and the fern fronds hung
in the rocky clefts; and the mountain mosses put on their
brightest green-velvet dress; and the wild iris, fringing the
water courses, hung out its yellow flag. Heaven's sunshine
flooded down over the laughing earth; and the blue sea
sparkled; and the rivulets sang as they hasted to the shore.

Margaret stood at the threshold of her home, enjoying the
balmy air and the sounds of the sweet springtime. She could
not see the sunshine and the verdure, but she knew it was
there, and she felt glad in its unseen beauty. Presently she
heard steps and voices, and her husband and Dr. Doran came
up the hill to her side.

"His honor has brought us a letter, Madge," said Antony, as he invited Dr. Doran to enter his cottage.

"It is too warm and bright out here to allow us to go within," said that gentleman. "Bring out a stool for your wife, Antony, and I will sit here on this great grey rock."

The letter was from Mrs. Somerset, enclosed in one to Dr. Doran. Part of it ran thus:

"It may be during the coming summer I shall go to Miramore for a month. I should so like to see Glenderg again. The time I spent in that place has never faded from my thoughts; I learnt there the most precious knowledge which can be known—the meaning of those words, 'the Love of God.' One day when I was sitting by the bedside of my dear little granddaughter, watching her tossing in her feverishness and pain, I heard you reading aloud to yourself the concluding portion of the eighth chapter of the Epistle to the Romans—and in all her restlessness and delirium, the dear child heard you also. She repeated the words after you: 'Neither death, nor life . . . nor things present, nor things to come . . . shall be able to separate us from the Love of God, which is in Christ Jesus our Lord!' 'The Love of God' she said softly, 'surely that is more than enough for us all.' I went away from the cottage soon afterwards; and in a few days, as you know, her sweet life on earth was ended, and we could hear her voice no more, but the words haunted me. I had thought that I knew much about religion, and creeds, and faith; but my cold theories were utterly at fault here. I daresay, dear friends (you must let me call you so), you do not altogether understand what I mean by writing thus; but at least you will, I am sure, be able to rejoice with me that now, at last, I also know what is meant by that Love of God."

"It is not here nor there that the good that blessed wean did is to be reckoned up," said Margaret softly. "Look at Neil, now! The likes of him isn't in the town for good-heartedness, ever since last year."

"Yes," said Dr. Doran thoughtfully, "I have noticed how changed he is."

"Changed, is it? True for ye, sir, and ye may well say that word," remarked Antony. "Iver since we was boys together, I've counted him a black-hearted villain; but now I don't know who I'd put before him as a good man and true. And it's the truth it is!

"When Madge, here, was first struck with her sore sorra of darkness, sir," went on Antony after a pause, "I foun' a verse in my Bible which comforted her like. I've thought since that maybe it meant us poor creatures, with our unknowledgeableness and our fancies, as much as it meant the wanting of the eyesight. I'll fetch out the book, and perhaps ye'll agree with me, sir."

He entered his cottage and returned presently, bearing the calf-skin-covered Bible which Wavie and he had read from so often; he turned over its leaves to the forty-second chapter of Isaiah.

"This be's the verse, sir," he said, looking up to Dr. Doran's face. "I mind right well reading it to the wife the night afore the Queen of the Wave was wrecked," and Antony read, slowly and reverently: "I will bring the blind by a way that they knew not; I will lead them in paths that they have not known: I will make darkness light before them, and crooked things straight. These things will I do unto them, and will not forsake them."

"Ay, ay," said Margaret to herself; "there's many's the dark heart which the Lord has made light with His own brightness. And the sweetest ray He ever sent in the flesh to Glenderg was just our own dear Wavie."

More books from The Good and the Beautiful Library

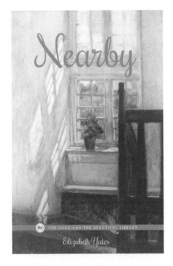

Nearby
by Elizabeth Yates

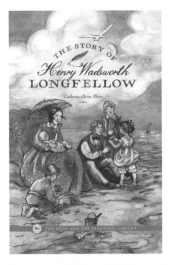

The Story of Henry Wadsworth Longfellow
by Francis E. Cook

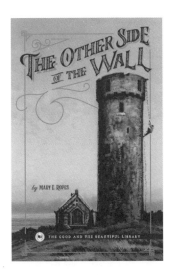

The Other Side of the Wall
by Catherine Owens Peare

The Good and the Beautiful Short Story Collection